FAMILY
ADVENTURES

CONWAY
Bloomsbury Publishing Plc
50 Bedford Square, London, WC1B 3DP, UK
29 Earlsfort Terrace, Dublin 2, Ireland

BLOOMSBURY, CONWAY and the Conway
logo are trademarks of Bloomsbury
Publishing Plc

First published in Great Britain 2024

This book is a guide for when you spend
time outdoors. Undertaking any activity
outdoors carries with it some risks that
cannot be entirely eliminated. For example,
you might get lost on a route or caught in bad
weather. Before you spend time outdoors,
we therefore advise that you always take the
necessary precautions, such as checking
weather forecasts and ensuring that you have
all the equipment you need. Any walking
routes that are described in this book
should not be relied upon as a sole means of
navigation, so we recommend that you refer
to an Ordnance Survey map or authoritative
equivalent.

This book may also reference businesses
and venues. Whilst every effort is made by
the author and the publisher to ensure the
accuracy of the business and venue information
contained in our books before they go to print,
changes to such information can occur during
the production and lifetime of a publication.
Therefore, we also advise that you check with
businesses or venues for the latest information
before setting out.

All internet addresses given in this book
were correct at the time of press.
Bloomsbury Publishing Plc does not have
any control over, or responsibility for, any
third-party websites referred to or in this
book. The author and the publisher regret
any inconvenience caused if some facts have
changed or sites have ceased to exist, but can
accept no responsibility for any such changes.

A catalogue record for this book is available
from the British Library
Library of Congress Cataloguing-in-Publication
data has been applied for

ISBN: PB: 978-1-8448-6659-5;
ePub: 978-1-8448-6658-8;
ePDF: 978-1-8448-6660-1

10 9 8 7 6 5 4 3 2 1

Typeset in IBM Plex Serif
Designed by Austin Taylor
Printed and bound in China by Toppan
Leefung Printing

To find out more about our authors and
books visit www.bloomsbury.com and
sign up for our newsletters

FAMILY ADVENTURES

HOW TO ADVENTURE WITH BABIES AND CHILDREN

BEX BAND

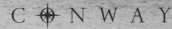
CONWAY
LONDON · OXFORD · NEW YORK · NEW DELHI · SYDNEY

CONTENTS

INTRODUCTION

CAMPING ADVENTURES

A NOTE ON SAFETY In this book, I've included lots of safety tips. It's impossible to cover every situation, so my suggestions are only intended as a guide. Before going on any adventure, you should conduct your research and risk assessments. Work well within your remit and capabilities, and always follow the safety guidelines for your intended activity. For more ideas on adventuring safely as a family, head to page 22.

TRAIL AND MOUNTAIN ADVENTURES

CYCLING ADVENTURES

WATER ADVENTURES

BIGGER ADVENTURES

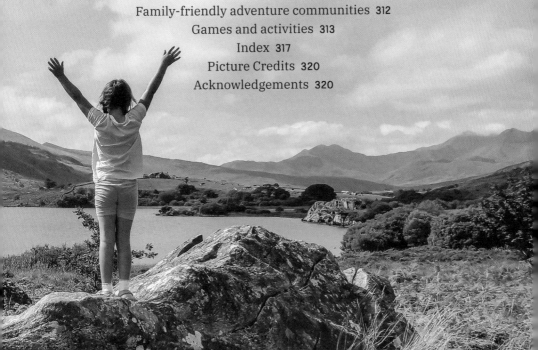

↗ On a big kick-scooting adventure, crossing Deception Pass Bridge in Washington, USA

INTRODUCTION

ADVENTURES, MY
FAMILY AND ME

It might not be very adventurous to admit it, but finishing is one of my favourite parts of any adventure. Or, more specifically, the moment you've had the hot shower and washed away all the dirt, put on a fresh set of clothes and sat down to put your feet up. My current seat was a bench outside a basic Bedouin tent in the heart of Israel's Negev desert. The bench was made from wooden crates with a worn, thin cushion on top. In normal circumstances, this would have been an exceptionally uncomfortable seat, but after days spent hiking and camping in the desert, it felt as luxurious as a sofa.

My daughter, Rivi, and husband, Gil, were just in sight on the edge of the Bedouin camp. He'd taken her to visit the resident camel, who was currently passed out on the floor resting after a long day in the sun. On the horizon, those deep oranges of a desert sunset were just beginning to show.

I love this part of an adventure because it's the moment I get to soak up the magnitude of what we've done and acknowledge the shift it's given me internally. In that instant, I felt an overriding emotion: contentment.

This had been a huge adventure for us, our biggest one yet as a family. It felt very fitting to make this happen here, where our love for adventure was formed, on the Israel National Trail. It also, in a way, felt like the end of a chapter as parents. Our daughter was reaching two years of age. Those first couple of years as parents are the hardest as you adjust to your new role and the madness that an infant brings. We'd been determined to make it count and to find a way to be the adventurous family we dreamed we would be. It had been a long journey, with a lot of learning along the way, but here we were, having completed an adventure that I would've

←« One of our biggest adventures before having kids. We spent three months kick-scooting the length of the USA

thought impossible when I was holding my newborn in those early weeks.

I stood up from the bench and stretched, every inch of my body stiff from the hiking. I called out to Gil; I was ready for the last step that made finishing an adventure so sweet ... dinner! I knew exactly what we'd be chatting about while we tucked into our evening feast.

What family adventure comes next?!

DECIDING TO START A FAMILY

'Having a baby will be your adventure now!'

Although it was well-meaning, every time someone said this during my first pregnancy, my reaction was not one of anticipation and excitement ... it just made me want to cry. Caring for babies didn't feel very adventurous to me; it felt like the complete opposite in many ways. I braced myself for losing much of my freedom, quiet, movement and exploration; all the things I associated with and loved about outdoor adventures. Despite the inevitable change that was heading my way, I still truly believed that I could have both: a family and an adventurous life. In the same way, I was hopeful that having children wouldn't mean letting go entirely of my much-loved career. But the narrative we kept being fed was telling me otherwise. People kept warning us that we wouldn't be able to travel any more or would give us that slightly patronising 'you'll see' look if we dared to mention our plans to continue camping or hiking once the baby had arrived.

←« Sat in our tent watching a volcano erupt while on a two-day hike on Acatenango, Guatemala

↗ Kick-scooting the length of the USA, from Canada to Mexico

On falling pregnant, we were handed piles of leaflets and books on how to keep your child safe at home, but when I searched, I could barely find anything on sleeping in a tent with an infant or managing day hikes with children. Activity suggestions varied from crafts in the home to games in the garden, but what about paddling on lakes or family cycling trips? I trawled books and the internet looking for inspiration from other families getting outdoors with children, and while there were some, the role models were few and far between.

I found the one-size-fits-all family lifestyle we're sold restrictive and knew it wouldn't work for us. Getting outdoors wasn't something I was willing to compromise on. For me and Gil, it was a necessity. A passion that identified us both and a remedy for all of life's stresses.

Having a baby might be our next adventure ... but there was no way it was going to be our only one!

IT WASN'T ALWAYS LIKE THIS

Outdoor adventures (which I define as anything involving getting physically active in the outdoors) had become a huge part of my life in the years before my daughter arrived. It hadn't always been that way, though. I was born to a large, concrete-laden town to an un-outdoorsy family. As a child, I had an aversion to physical activity, which continued into my adult years when I moved to London.

Despite my lack of experience in camping and hiking, in my late twenties, I made the bold and rash decision that I wanted to hike the Israel National Trail with Gil. It's a 1,000km (160 mile)-long trek that snakes the length of Gil's home country, Israel, and includes crossing the vast Negev desert. The decision to pack down our city life to hike the trail was driven by unhappiness. I desperately sought change and a path in life that didn't grind me down with disconnect, endless commutes and dissatisfying jobs.

Although I didn't know exactly what I was looking for, our big hiking adventure delivered the change I sought. After two months on the trail, I left feeling more confident and surer of who I was and who I wanted to be. It also left me with a new passion for the outdoors.

My trail experience gave me an idea for a new project. I'd barely met any women on the courses I'd joined in preparation for the hike, and not a single one doing the trail, so I created a Facebook group called Love Her Wild, launching a women's adventure community. What started as a small online group grew over several years into a thriving non-profit and one of the largest outdoor communities in the world, providing support, initiatives and exciting women-only adventures to thousands. In the process, I built a career and a name for myself around my new love of outdoor adventures and conservation. When I wasn't running the Love Her Wild community and leading expeditions, I was writing about adventure in blogs and books or talking about them on stage.

Gil had an equally life-changing experience. Leaving his big corpo-

⚑ Practising navigation (and getting lost) while hiking in UK National Parks

rate job in London, he retrained and became an expedition leader and freelance marketer, then later a freediving instructor. Our lives and how we chose to spend our free time were unrecognisable from those of the young adults who left London. No matter how busy we become in our careers now, we always find time to get outdoors – from evening walks and weekend camping trips to big, epic adventures such as kick-scooting the length of the USA or kayaking the width of the UK. Our life felt wholesome, dynamic, exciting and full of travel.

Despite how happy and fulfilled we were with our lives, there was still another dream we wanted to make happen ... becoming parents! Although we weren't naive about the fact that life would change and we'd have to let go of a lot of the freedom we had at the time, we also weren't willing to listen to the naysayers who claimed we wouldn't be able to continue adventuring as a family. It was a passion and a necessity in our lives that we just weren't willing to compromise on.

WELCOMING RIVI

My beautiful daughter arrived into the world at home on a warm summer's day. While we hid inside in our deliciously sleepy newborn bubble, the world outside was in a state of mayhem and confusion as we were tentatively stepping out of our first national Covid-19 lockdown.

←« Kayaking the width of the UK, from Bristol to London via waterways

↘ Hiking in the Negev desert. About one month into our hike on the 1,000km-long Israel National Trail

Although I wouldn't wish having a baby during a pandemic on anyone (the anxiety, loneliness, uncertainty and isolation as a parent are brutal enough without throwing a pandemic into the mix!), there was one positive I can draw from becoming a parent during this strange time: our exploration and travel would have come to an abrupt halt during the restrictions regardless ... so in a way, it made the transition into our new family life that little bit easier.

The lockdowns forced us to take things slow, which I learned in time is an exceptionally good pace as a parent; you are very much in an ultra-marathon, not a sprint. We patiently waited for campsites and travel to reopen so we could take our initial tiny steps back into the outdoors, starting with camping and hiking, then moving on to water and cycling adventures. It was like beginning from scratch again, discovering what to pack, how to manage our unpredictable new teammate, and our new limits. The more we did, though, the more we grew in confidence, and our adventures got bigger and braver. The outdoors provided even more benefits to us now that we were parents, whose well-being and health were more fragile than ever. It brought calm even to the most exhausting, chaotic days.

Of course, our lives look very different now, and there's no point pretending you can continue adventuring as you would if you didn't have children. Children are high-risk, require a ridiculous amount of gear considering their size, and have lower thresholds and stamina. As a result, adventures will be smaller and fewer. You must constantly adapt and realise that most of your plans won't work out as you intend, and there will be times when it's just too much, and you pushed yourselves too far.

While Gil slotted into this new way of adventuring quickly, it was a bit of a process of acceptance for me. I don't think I'll ever stop missing the freedom we used to have and how easy it was just to pack a bag and head out into the hills. But for all that has been lost, much has been gained too. Introducing the outdoors to my daughter brings me great joy, as does the shared family time and the old cliché of being able to experience nature through the eyes of a child. I also really enjoy the creativity that comes with family adventures and the challenge of trying to make things work, even if, at first, they don't seem possible. I lean into this, knowing it won't be this way for ever.

FROM WILD CAMPING TO HOT TUBS

Parenting is hard. Your kids and society are beating you up enough as it is ... you don't need to be throwing extra punches your way! As you flick through this book, agree not to use it for comparison or a reason to feel like you're not doing enough. This book exists to give you ideas, make

the logistics of family adventuring a little bit easier, and provide some inspiration for when you're ready to stretch your wings a bit more.

The outdoors has become a huge part of our lives and careers, but don't let that put you off. This has only been a recent journey for us in the last seven-ish years. Underneath all our exciting journeys, we really are just ordinary people who still get imposter syndrome and doubt our fitness before *every* adventure. I'd hate for anyone to pick up this book and feel like they aren't adventurous enough or they can't compete, because the outdoors is for everyone, and there is no comparison in mother nature.

I want this book to be a confidence boost. While logistics and planning are challenging, these are skills you'll hone with time (like nappy changing and school runs). A lack of confidence is often the real barrier stopping parents and carers from getting outdoors more. Taking small, brave steps, trusting your instincts and believing you are capable will slowly build your confidence over time.

I'll share our journey of returning to adventuring as a family, along with stories from other families who have successfully made the outdoors a part of their lives. You'll find the families and their chosen activities vary greatly – from parents and carers who, like me, were adventurous before they had children, to parents and carers who only started taking their first steps into the outdoors after having kids. Some families do big, long-distance adventures, wild camping along the way. Some families do smaller day challenges or go on simple and comfortable adventures.

It doesn't matter which stories you most relate to or how experienced you are in the outdoors. There is no right or wrong way to go on adventures. You also don't have to pigeonhole yourself to one type. The outdoor world can be oppressively competitive and judgemental – it was shying away from this attitude that inspired me to set up Love Her Wild in the first place. Adventures are much more enjoyable and beneficial when you take away expectations. I love doing the big adventures we've taken on as a family – the ones where you carry all your food, camp alone in the wilderness and don't shower for days. Sometimes I also love to be warm and comfortable, though. I might want to get away, but don't have the energy or inclination to do anything grand, so we opt for a comfortable glamping site instead (oh, what a surprise ... who knew it came with a hot tub?!).

The why and how don't matter. What matters is getting outdoors and being close to nature. Raising children is a messy, exhausting juggling act, and it can be easy to avoid adding additional challenges when you are simply trying to get through your days. But getting outdoors, in any capacity, is a fight worth having. Even more so when you feel like you are in survival mode. The long-term benefits will enrich your family like nothing else, leaving you healthier, more resilient and brimming with a lifetime of memories.

MEET OUR FAMILY!

Our family adventures in this book span several years. My niece and nephew also join many of our journeys. We love that the outdoors is something we can bring to their lives too (and, of course, that it makes us the cool auntie and uncle!). From our experience, throwing extra children into the mix doesn't make a massive difference and can even sometimes result in spare free time when they play together. Are there other children you can award the gift of adventure to in your life?

This is us as we are now:

BEX
(mum/auntie)

RIVI
(daughter, aged two)

GIL
(dad/uncle)

DULCIE
(niece, aged nine)

COOPER
(nephew, aged six)

ADVENTURING WITH CHILDREN

HOW FAR CAN CHILDREN HIKE?

Although distances vary greatly depending on the individual child
(and perhaps most notably, willingness on that particular day),
generally, children can hike between 0.8km (½ mile) and 1.6km (1 mile)
per year of their age. These distances may increase if a child is hiking
regularly but would decrease considerably if the terrain or weather
were challenging.

HOW FAR CAN CHILDREN WALK?

Age	Distance
2–3	1.6–4.8km (1–3 miles)
4–5	3.2–8km (2–5 miles)
6–7	4.8–11.3km (3–7 miles)
8–9	6.4–14.5km (4–9 miles)
10+	16km+ (10+ miles)

A note on carriers and off-road buggies: Hiking carriers and off-road
buggies often have an upper weight limit of 22kg (48.5lb), which means
you can carry or do a walk/carry combo until around five to six years of age.

HOW MUCH WEIGHT CAN CHILDREN CARRY?

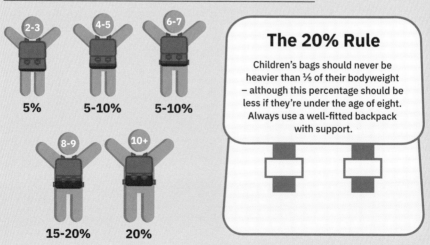

2-3 — 5%

4-5 — 5-10%

6-7 — 5-10%

8-9 — 15-20%

10+ — 20%

The 20% Rule

Children's bags should never be
heavier than ⅕ of their bodyweight
– although this percentage should be
less if they're under the age of eight.
Always use a well-fitted backpack
with support.

RECOMMENDED AGES FOR STARTING OUTDOOR SPORTS

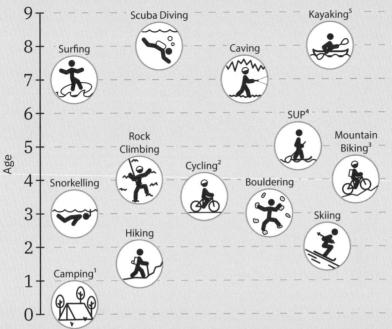

[1] 2 months; [2] 6 months in child seat; [3] 2–5 years in child seat; [4] 2–5 years on adult SUP; [5] 4 years in tandem

HOW FAR CAN CHILDREN CYCLE?

Generally, children can cycle around 1.6km (1 mile) per year of their age. This will vary depending on the terrain, weather and concentration abilities of the child. Assume an average cycling speed for children aged 5–10 of 16km/h (10mph).

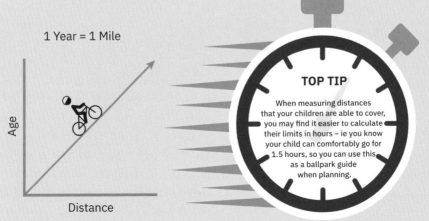

1 Year = 1 Mile

Age

Distance

TOP TIP

When measuring distances that your children are able to cover, you may find it easier to calculate their limits in hours – ie you know your child can comfortably go for 1.5 hours, so you can use this as a ballpark guide when planning.

BEING SAFE

OUTDOORS WITH

CHILDREN

Safety is a massive consideration for any adventure and should always be your number one priority. While I include some tips below and later in the book in regard to specific activities, it's vital that you carry out your own research and risk assessment before participating in any adventurous activity.

Most parents and carers will intuitively be over-cautious. Being over-cautious is a good approach, as you never want to take unnecessary risks, especially when children are involved.

THINGS TO BEAR IN MIND

WORK WELL WITHIN YOUR REMIT

Be honest about your experience, knowledge and skills. While it's OK to challenge yourself when going on an adventure, when it involves children, everything you do should be well within the abilities of the adults in charge.

BUILD YOUR SKILLS

Going on courses can be a great way to build your skills. I'd highly recommend that all adults in your party, as a minimum, do at least an introductory first aid course (with paediatrics included). Navigation

⬆ Enjoying local family hikes in Somerset all year round

skills could save your life, as can a water management course if you plan to do any water-based activities.

DO YOUR RESEARCH

Before heading out, ensure you've conducted extensive research on all areas that might impact your adventure. That includes knowing your routes, where your get-outs are and where help is if you need it. It also means having regular, up-to-date information on weather forecasts. Poor weather can be lethal and should never be underestimated.

HAVE THE CORRECT KIT

Different activities will require different kit and safety equipment – such as a helmet for cycling or a buoyancy aid for paddling. As a general rule, though, you should always carry spare warm clothes and waterproofs (for all the family), a map and compass, plenty of food and water, a torch, a first aid kit, a fully charged phone and a battery pack (in a waterproof bag), a whistle and survival bag/shelter. Safety gear should always be age-appropriate and fitted correctly according to instructions.

DRESS YOUR CHILDREN LIKE A CHRISTMAS TREE

Make sure your children are bright and visible, so they are easy to see. Opt for a bright red coat over a black one or give them all fluorescent beanies.

GIVE YOUR CHILDREN AUTONOMY

If you constantly instruct your children, not only will they switch off and stop listening, but you will also not be teaching them to become problem-solving thinkers in the outdoors. Give children the freedom to try things, make (safe) mistakes and lead. Only give feedback or instructions when it is really needed.

TELL SOMEONE WHERE YOU'RE GOING

Make sure someone knows your intended route and how long you're expected to be away. Ideally, you should check in with this person once a day to let them know you're all fine. This way, you have someone to alert the authorities if something goes wrong, and you aren't able to call for help yourself.

RUN THROUGH WORSE-CASE SCENARIOS

As part of your adventure planning, you should set aside time to run through different scenarios – a child getting lost, someone getting injured, arriving at the wild camping spot late and realising it's not suitable, etc. Have a clear plan for how you can reduce the risk of these happening and what you will do if something does go wrong. Know how and who to call to help. What3Words (www.what3words.com) is a great app to have on your phone – it can assist emergency services in finding your location quickly and is simple enough for children to use too.

EQUIP YOUR CHILDREN

Children are often more capable than we give them credit for. Before any adventure, do practice scenarios, so they know what to do if someone gets injured or they get lost.

Each child should have a warm item of clothing, a snack, a torch and a whistle on them either in a bag or in pockets. If they get lost and

←« »→ Using our Osprey Poco child carrier
while on a local hike

separated, teach them that they should put on all their warm layers and use their whistles. It's vital that they stay still until they are found and don't start walking to try to find you … this will likely lead to them getting more lost. They should also know where you keep your phone and how to call the emergency services in case their supervising adult is injured or can't help.

KNOW WHEN TO STOP

Quitting can be tough, but it's an essential skill for adventuring and staying safe. If the weather turns, the terrain is more challenging than you anticipated or someone is struggling, never be tempted to push through. There is never any shame in turning around.

BOOK AN EXPERT

If you are ever in doubt or feeling unsure, book an expert. There are many great leaders and instructors out there who can help you plan and deliver a suitable family adventure.

LET'S TALK COWS

You wouldn't believe the number of times cows get brought up when I ask people what's stopping them from getting outdoors more! I get it. They're big and confusing. Sometimes I look into their eyes and see a gentle soul, and other times (usually when they're making a beeline for me), I think they're determined to kill me.

🚶 Muddy walks on our glamping family adventure

🔦 Storytime in our bell tent. We always pack a couple of books on our adventures to encourage quiet moments like this

Most cows will not cause harm but check for bulls or mothers and calves before entering a field. You'll want to give them a wide birth and never get between a mother and its calf. Stick to the edge of the field, and cross quietly and swiftly. Avoid running or making lots of noise – this will usually pique their interest! If they do start approaching you, it's usually just because they are curious or think you have food. Most cows will stop a few metres from you and won't get any closer.

SAFE WATER: PURIFYING OUTDOORS

For most day-long activities, you'll probably be able to take enough drinking water with you. For overnight adventures or if you are carrying a lot of heavy gear, it may be necessary to collect and purify water while outdoors.

Before your trip, do your research so you know what the best water sources are in the area. You might pass a pub or petrol station where you can access a tap. If you are more rural, streams and rivers will be your best source – always preferable over still water, which could be stagnant.

Generally, the higher up you collect the water, the less likely it is to be contaminated, so you might want to factor this in when planning.

Ideally, water needs to be collected from a section of water that is fast-moving, where the water looks very clear. Bottles with wide lids – such as Nalgene bottles – are best for this. You'll likely accidentally collect a few small bits of debris or bugs in your bottle; if there's a huge amount, pour the water back into the stream or river and try collecting from a different area. Alternatively, if you take a muslin cloth cut into a small square, you can place it over the lid of the bottle, where it will filter any debris.

While some adults are comfortable drinking straight from fast-moving water without sterilising it first, you should never take this risk with children, pregnant women, older adults and people with weakened immune systems. Once collected, there are then four ways you can sterilise water:

1   **Boiling:** Bring the water to a full rolling boil for at least 1 minute, then allow it to cool fully before drinking. At elevations above 2,000m (6,562ft), boil it for at least 3 minutes. This process can take a long time and requires a stove and gas.

2   **Disinfecting:** You can add disinfecting tablets to your water to kill bacteria. They are usually cheap and easy to use, taking about 30 minutes to work. The downside is that they are chemical-based, which some might want to avoid, and often leave a taste in your water (check that your children will drink it in advance if using this method).

3   **Filtration:** Filtration systems are usually straws or attachments that are added to your water bottle or hydration bladder, which filter the water as you drink. They are easy to use and don't leave a taste, although some require you to suck harder to get the water out, which might be tricky for small children. Filtration systems tend to be more expensive, and the filters must be replaced regularly.

4   **UV sterilisation:** These UV devices destroy bacteria in the water. They are usually a straw shape, which you hold in your water bottle for a set amount of time with the UV on. There are now also bottles on the market – like our go-to for water sterilisation, LARQ Bottle PureVis (www.livelarq.com) – which have UV sterilising technology conveniently fitted in the lid. You can use one as a central purifier before distributing it to other bottles. These devices are usually very pricey and require charging.

TIPS FOR SUCCESSFUL

FAMILY ADVENTURES

Adventuring with children is very different from when you are managing a trip with just adults. Packing, logistics, managing distances and food intake – it's all different. It took us a while to get the balance right and to realise where the struggles would come from and what to let go of.

EXPECT THINGS NOT TO WORK OUT AS PLANNED

We've yet to have a family adventure that has gone entirely to plan! Usually, this has resulted in cutting the adventure short or changing the plan because we overestimated our/the children's stamina or the distance we can cover. Before setting off, have a plan B ... and also a plan C... in place. This will make it much easier to adapt and still make a success of the adventure if (when!) things don't go to plan.

≫→ Getting children to help with tasks like setting up camp is a great way to get them involved and feel more engaged with your adventures

LESS IS MORE

This has been our biggest learning experience. While we used to love a complex and challenging adventure, with children in tow it really is the case that less is more. A simple plan, with lots of downtime factored in and logistics that won't make your brain melt is a recipe for success. Shorten the distance you expect to travel ... and then shorten it again.

Over the last few years, I've learned to let go of the idea that we needed to travel far to have a sense of wilderness and adventure. Even trekking a mile into a national park can give you stunning scenery and a sense of being far from civilisation.

PRINT YOUR PACKING LISTS

They might be small, but, my goodness, children can need a lot of stuff! This is especially true if travelling with infants. We've made a habit of printing our packing lists (and updating them after every adventure). This makes the packing process *so* much easier the next time and means you're less likely to forget something vital.

IT'S WORTH THE EFFORT

A common theme with all my family adventures is that I get to the moment of leaving, then I suddenly have a strong sense that I don't want to do it any more. After hours of planning and packing, all while juggling an anxious, over-excited child, I'm tired. I want to crawl into my bed and do nothing. As soon as I start the adventure, though, that all melts away. I always find that parenting is much easier on an adventure away from house chores and work, and I find myself relaxed and enjoying the moment. The effort is worth it, I promise!

LET GO OF THE IDEA OF ENTERTAINMENT

We're obsessed in Western cultures with entertaining our children but, left to be bored for a bit, children will soon make up their own games. This is especially so outside. The more you practise this, the longer they will be able to play outdoors unaided. Don't worry about bringing toys or screens; trust that sticks, rocks and streams will provide all the entertainment they need.

GET THE CHILDREN INVOLVED IN EVERYTHING YOU DO

Getting older kids involved in planning and choosing routes will make them much more engaged with the adventure. Teach them how to navigate and trust them to lead easy stretches. At the campsite, let them help set up the tent or light a fire (even if it takes longer) – even better if you can

⅄ Camping and adventuring with children often comes with extra baggage!

⬆ Have a few games up your sleeve for when your children get tired on walks

let them work it out themselves with minimal/no instruction. Children thrive off feeling independent and having autonomy, and remember that this supports them in becoming problem-solving and capable individuals in the outdoors.

STICK TO YOUR USUAL ROUTINES (ALTHOUGH MAYBE NOT FOR DAY ONE)

As much as possible, we stick to our usual sleep and food routines that we have at home. This helps keep the children happy, rested and feeling secure. The exception is the first day when there's usually way too much excitement to get any small person rested and well-fed. So, on the first night, we let the children run wild until they crash!

Lack of sleep and fatigue can be a big enemy in the outdoors for all the family. Make sure you factor in plenty of rest time and breaks, and ensuring everyone is sleeping well will help keep morale and energy up.

REMEMBER, IT'S YOUR ADVENTURE TOO

While it might not be the adventure you would choose if you didn't have children, it's important to remember that it's still for you as much as for them. We only go on adventures that we want to do ourselves. To places we want to visit, doing activities that we want to enjoy. That way, we also take enjoyment and satisfaction away from experience. Remember, it's a *family* adventure, so your enjoyment is just as valid and important as the children's.

THROW MORE ADULTS INTO THE MIX

If you have the luxury of bringing a patient friend or family member on your adventure with you, this can massively reduce the load – both physically carrying the gear but also emotionally managing childcare and helping with tasks.

A better idea might be to go on an adventure with another family – the same way the Somerset and Pearson-Smith family joined together for a cycle tour in France (see page 194). The adults will understand the slow pace and disruption children are likely to bring to your adventure. Although not always easy – throwing more

⤒ A winter escape in a picturesque off-grid cabin in the woods

children into the mix and merging with differing family styles can cause conflict – if successful, it could enable you to pool your energies and expertise to go on more ambitious adventures while sharing great memories with good friends.

A WALK TURNED RUN ON THE DALES WAY

by Tim Moss
....

@nextchallenge | www.thenextchallenge.org

BEFORE WE HAD KIDS, 'adventuring' was our default use of all annual leave and most weekends. Our trips ranged from a three-day crossing of the Wahiba Sands desert in Oman to a 16-month round-the-world cycle; and from running the length of every London Underground line to walking across frozen Lake Baikal in Siberia.

We did a mixture of big trips, which were only occasionally achievable, with lots of smaller projects that could fit around work commitments. That included trying to swim the Thames over many separate weekends and a week's holiday crossing Ibiza on foot.

There was never any doubt that our adventuring would continue with kids. Not because we are out to prove anything but because we love it and it's a big part of our lives. This has, of course, meant approaching our adventures differently. We've never been great at detailed trip planning, preferring instead to wing it (carefully sold as the idea of 'remaining open to opportunity'). As parents, though, we have to plan a bit more to consider the need for diversions and rest stops, although we now assume that whatever plans we make will need to change at some point.

Staying open to adapting and changing the plan has been vital for making our family adventures a success. Our attempt to hike the Dales Way demonstrated this perfectly.

THE DALES WAY

The Dales Way footpath is 125km (78 miles) long and mostly follows riverside paths and gentle foothills, and passes through the heart of the Yorkshire Dales. The start of the Dales Way was close to our house at the time in Yorkshire, with the end passing by our future home in the South Lakes. It felt like a symbolic gesture.

This winter adventure allowed us to fit in one more long-distance walking trip before our first son grew too big to carry. At 14 months old, he was still small enough to lug about in a baby carrier rucksack.

We completed the first section from Ilkley to Bolton Abbey on a weekend prior to the main event and broke the rest of the trail into nine days/sections:

1. **Bolton Abbey** – Grassington (13.5km/8.4 miles)
2. **Grassington** – Starbotton (13.4km/8.3 miles)
3. **Starbotton** – Oughtershaw (13.8km/8.6 miles)
4. **Oughtershaw** – Gearstones (9.5km/5.9 miles)
5. **Gearstones** – Dent (15km/9.3 miles)
6. **Dent** – Lincoln's Inn Bridge (Sedbergh) (13.2km/8.2 miles)
7. **Lincoln's Inn Bridge** (Sedbergh) – Meal Bank (14.5km/9 miles)
8. **Meal Bank** – Staveley (10.5km/6.5 miles)
9. **Staveley** – Bowness (10.5km/6.5 miles)

Our daily mileage gave us plenty of time for rest stops to give our son a break from his carrier, but it still felt like we were getting a reasonable day's walking in.

For the first couple of days, we were able to get the bus back to the start each afternoon, meaning we could have an evening at home and a night in our own bed. We didn't want to camp on this trip, as we had enough to carry with a child on one of our backs without having to haul winter camping kit as well. So when bus links weren't possible, we stopped in B&Bs along the way.

It meant we could get by with just a 35-litre rucksack between us, along with the baby carrier rucksack we were using, which had ample space underneath the base, which we used for bulky, lightweight things, such as nappies.

COLD AND A COLD

One of the biggest problems we faced was keeping our boy warm enough when he was in the back of a rucksack for a full day. We walk a lot as a family, and usually, we'd be able to stop in a cafe to warm up or abandon a plan and head back home. That wasn't possible this time: there were few cafes, and we needed to push on each day, to reach that night's accommodation. The temperatures were consistently below zero, so we put extra layers of baby and adult socks on his feet instead of his usual wellies.

Halfway through the trip, we felt like terrible parents for putting our boy through several days of sub-zero temperatures. This feeling was only exacerbated when he developed a horrible cold. So, as we reached the high point of the route, near Oughtershaw, we stopped in that night's farmhouse accommodation and decided to change the plan.

To give our son a rest, we converted our family walking holiday into a solo running holiday: in the mornings, one of us would run the day's route while the other did the childcare, and then we'd switch roles in the afternoon. This plan required a car, but our route took us past Ribblehead railway station the next day so we could nip home on the train to get it.

For the journey's second half, our tag-team system allowed us to continue with the adventure, just in a different way than initially planned. Each of us took turns running sections of the route. Laura (my wife) would run a few miles while I drove ahead to the next village. On arrival, Laura would jump in the car and drive me back to the start so that I could have a turn running the route.

What began as a family walking holiday turned into an endurance event during which we spent most of the day alone, running through some of the wildest and most beautiful landscapes Yorkshire has to offer. We would reconvene each afternoon to cook dinner and monitor our son as he practised his newly developed walking skills.

It might not have been our original plan, but it turned into a brilliant, albeit slightly weird, holiday. With children, it's so rare to find time alone, and having a couple of hours to ourselves in the hills every day was a luxury and a privilege. It was also nice to have a couple of one-on-one hours with our little boy each day, giving him our full attention.

ADVENTURING WITH KIDS

Our adventuring has definitely changed – Laura is now pregnant with our third child. Generally, we've done less long-distance walking and camping because it's hard carrying kit and kids (although plenty of parents still do that, such as our friends Neil and Harriet Pike – @pikesonbikes) and more cycle touring. From trailers at six months old to some combination of front seats, back seats, crossbar saddles, balance bikes and follow-me tandems, cycling is a great way to have an adventure with young kids. We cycled up the Baltic coast to the Åland Islands while our first was still a baby. And we've cycled across Scotland to Shetland and Orkney, along some of Ireland's greenways and down

Ardnamurchan, with two kids in tow.

We've found adventuring with kids involves more faff and less mileage, but the ultimate experience is the same. Our kids love it too because they get so much attention. We've also discovered that camping is good with kids. There's more space to burn off energy and make the kind of racket that would get you kicked out of a restaurant or hotel, and there is plenty of novelty to keep them entertained (camping mats! headtorches! tents! stoves!). The same goes for wild camping. We were daunted the first time we did it, but in some ways, it's easier than a campsite. You've got everything you need within arm's reach and don't have to worry about other campers or trekking to the toilets.

Never feel like you can't do stuff just because you've got kids. It will be tougher, take longer and involve a lot more faff, but you can absolutely still get outside and have adventures.

That said, because adventuring – and life in general – is harder when kids are involved, don't beat yourself up if you can't do as much as you did before. Make your life easier when you can: take the shorter route, avoid the rain, drive to the start, go for the occasional cafe/hotel rather than picnic and campsites all the time. Let go of any rigid ideas of how an adventure should be and instead just focus on getting out there, no matter how many adaptations you need to make along the way!

DRESSING FOR
ADVENTURE

Dressing correctly for the outdoors is a crucial step to get right. If dressed well, everyone stays warm, dry, happy and comfortable.

When adventuring in the UK, I think the 'outer layer' explained below is the most crucial step to get right with your children (warm layers are also important but easier to adjust with a cheap extra fleece thrown on). Rain can fall at any time of the year, and being able to shield your children from the elements well ultimately means more time spent outdoors, no matter the weather. For this reason, I've always prioritised investing in good-quality waterproofs over anything else!

Which material is best?

COTTON: Cheap and readily available. It's slow to dry though and doesn't feel warm when wet. Cotton is fine for short outings in mild weather but isn't ideal.

SYNTHETIC: Mid-range cost and relatively easy to find. It dries quickly and is durable. Ideal for long adventures and cold weather.

WOOL: Expensive and not so readily available. Stays warm when wet and is odour-resistant – the most effective material for more extended and colder adventures.

When dressing for the outdoors, you need to think of the three-layering system. This consists of a base layer, a mid-layer and an outer layer. You can easily add and take off layers – removing when you get warm or adding a layer when you stop for a break and start feeling cold.

Unless you are taking an infant who is being carried (and therefore not moving much), as much as possible, you want everyone to dress so they

Base layer

This is the layer you wear against your skin, wicking sweat from your body so you stay dry. A T-shirt on top and shorts on the bottom will be enough in warmer weather. In cold weather, long johns and a long-sleeved top is preferred. When camping, base layers make ideal pyjamas.

Mid-layer

Provides an insulating layer. A low-cost pull-on fleece and walking trousers work well in most weather. An extra fleece can be great to have as a spare if needed. For colder weather, a synthetic puffer jacket is a light and versatile item that can provide a surprising amount of warmth.

are just slightly cold when starting out. When you start moving, whether walking, cycling or paddling, your body heat will increase, making you feel warmer. If you begin with too many layers, just ten minutes after starting you'll all have to stop to remove layers.

No one should be sweating in their clothes. If you sweat, you'll make them wet, and they'll stop being effective at insulating you. Stop and remove a layer as soon as you or your children start sweating.

ADDITIONAL ACCESSORIES

Accessories can help to keep your extremes warm or add a little bit of warmth when a jumper or coat is too much. A buff can be used as a scarf for extra warmth or pulled over your mouth and nose to protect you from the wind or cold. A hat and gloves will keep your head and hands warm.

Outer layer

The outer layer exists to protect you from the elements. Waterproof trousers (or salopettes) and a waterproof jacket will protect you from the wind and rain.

Top tips for dressing children for adventures

• **Socks make great gloves** for children ... they don't fall off so easily and are easier to put on and pull off.
• **Buy clothes one size up** for children so they last longer – cuffs can easily be rolled up. Look for adjustable waistbands on trousers.
• **Keep your spare clothes,** hats and gloves in dry bags (I always have one for adult items and one for children). That way they are organised, easy to find and protected from getting wet.

ONESIES

All-in-one fleeces, puffers (snowsuits) and waterproofs are readily available for children. While they make going to the toilet a little annoying, they are a great way to manage wet or cold weather and a quick way to get children outside without needing a full outfit change.

We've always packed our trusted Töastie Kids (www.toastiekids.com) onesies with us, whatever the adventure, and even used the Töastie Kids puffer as an alternative to a toddler sleeping bag.

SHOES AND SOCKS

Just like adults, children need to be wearing comfortable footwear to enjoy hiking. While wellies are fine for short romps, if you are hoping to do regular hiking, you should buy proper shoes or boots and get their feet regularly measured so they are the right fit.

Hiking or sports socks will keep their feet dry and comfortable – a thick wool or synthetic pair for winter and a thinner pair for summer. Never use cotton socks, as this increases the chances of developing blisters.

←« ↕ Töastie Kids offers a great range of onesies which are perfect for getting outdoors with babies and toddlers

FEEDING THE FAMILY
ON AN ADVENTURE

While writing this book, I kept joking that all my adventuring with kids advice could pretty much be summarised in one sentence: 'snacks, snacks and more snacks!'

Food is everything on an adventure. Even when I adventure alone, I often turn to food for motivation and comfort. It's also your fuel. The thing that will keep your energy levels up and morale in check.

Food is even more critical when you involve children because their stamina, willpower and ability to control emotions are not as advanced as those of an adult.

←« »→ Cooking and eating outdoors is one of our favourite things to do as a family. We have a fire pit in our garden, which encourages us to keep this up at home throughout the year

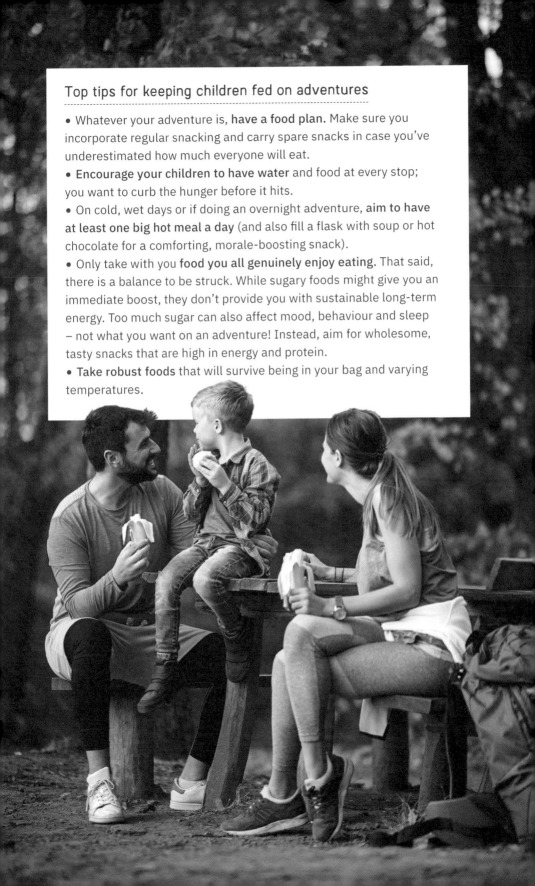

Top tips for keeping children fed on adventures

- Whatever your adventure is, **have a food plan.** Make sure you incorporate regular snacking and carry spare snacks in case you've underestimated how much everyone will eat.
- **Encourage your children to have water** and food at every stop; you want to curb the hunger before it hits.
- On cold, wet days or if doing an overnight adventure, **aim to have at least one big hot meal a day** (and also fill a flask with soup or hot chocolate for a comforting, morale-boosting snack).
- Only take with you **food you all genuinely enjoy eating.** That said, there is a balance to be struck. While sugary foods might give you an immediate boost, they don't provide you with sustainable long-term energy. Too much sugar can also affect mood, behaviour and sleep – not what you want on an adventure! Instead, aim for wholesome, tasty snacks that are high in energy and protein.
- **Take robust foods** that will survive being in your bag and varying temperatures.

↑ Food for a four-day hiking and wild camping adventure in Dartmoor. This covered meals and snacks for two adults and a baby

⤳ Expedition food packs are a great lightweight option for meals when on an adventure

SNACK SUGGESTIONS

Here are some of our favourite snacks to take out and about:

- whole-grain crackers (add nut butter, or chunks of cheese if needed)
- whole-grain breadsticks
- unsweetened cereal
- thick pancakes (make at home and take with you)
- dried fruit and nuts
- sliced fresh fruit or veg
- flapjacks
- malt loaf

- home-made whole-grain muffins (could be made sweet with blueberries or savoury with sun-dried tomatoes, olives and cheese)
- energy balls (great to make at home with your favourite fruit, nuts and flavourings)
- popcorn (not very high in energy but keeps children entertained!)
- jerky
- nut butters (buy in sachets to be squeezed into your mouth)
- nutritious snack bars
- baby food in pouches (these might be enjoyed by older children as much as babies!)

MEAL SUGGESTIONS

For most of our main meals on adventures, we rely on pouched food, which is easy to carry, lightweight and easy to cook. Supermarkets now sell a huge range of tasty pouched meals that are quick to reheat, from rice, couscous, lentils to curries and stews. Here are some ideas:

- cereal or porridge with dried fruit for breakfast (use water, milk powder or UHT milk sachets)
- sandwiches (rye bread, pitta or wraps are most sturdy. Marmite, nut butter or chocolate spread make good fillings)
- pasta and sauce (buy a pre-made sauce in a pouch)
- rice pouch (buy pre-cooked in a pouch – different flavours are available)
- dhal and lentils in a pouch
- just-add-water pre-seasoned couscous
- sachet of baked beans with some crackers
- dehydrated meals (can be bought from outdoor stores or made yourself at home using a dehydrator machine)
- instant custard
- home-made flapjacks

ADVENTURING WITH
BABIES AND TODDLERS

Undoubtedly, it is easier to get out adventuring with your children as they get older. However, the effort involved in getting outdoors with infants and toddlers shouldn't stop you. The reality is that they are hard work even at home, and, once you've got the planning and logistics finished and are on your way, adventure life with a small person can feel surprisingly easy; they are often happier and more relaxed outside ... as are you, away from all the external pressures.

At this age, though, children are most vulnerable to the elements, so you really shouldn't be taking any unnecessary risks or pushing yourself beyond your or their capabilities.

⚑ Teaching Rivi how to start a fire at Nature's Nest glamping site in the Wye Valley

INFANTS AND EXTREME TEMPERATURES

Infants cannot regulate their body temperature like an older child or adult can. You must be especially cautious in extreme temperatures if you are getting outdoors with a baby. The best decision might be to give up on your plans for another day when the weather is milder.

When outdoors, check your infant's neck and chest regularly – if the skin feels hot and clammy and your baby is red-faced and looks uncomfortable, this is a sign they are too hot. If they feel cold, are shivering and look pale, they are too cold.

Cuddling your baby against your skin will warm them up, as will getting them active and moving about. It's more effective to add extra layers after warming them up first.

You can cool down a baby by stripping off layers and placing damp towels over them. Make sure you get liquids into them quickly, either milk or water.

NAPPIES OUTDOORS

Getting out with Rivi when she was still in nappies was a faff, and significantly increased the amount of stuff we needed to carry. At home, we use cloth nappies and wipes. We would continue with our cloth nappies as usual for day outings and take a dry bag to put used ones in to carry back.

For longer trips, it is possible to continue with cloth nappies. This is easier in drier weather. Once you've changed your child's nappy, hang the nappy and wipe out to dry either on your pack or around camp if you have stopped for the day (dispose of any poo as you would adults' by digging a hole 15cm/6in deep and away from water sources). You don't want to carry wet used nappies as they are soaked with urine and heavy.

If you are lucky enough to have a water source nearby, you can rinse them straightaway. Otherwise, you'll need to dry them dirty and wait until this is possible.

The all-in-two nappies work best for this system – where you have an absorbent inner layer and a separate outer waterproof 'shell', which can be used for multiple changes before needing to be cleaned. All-in-one nappies (where the inner cloth and waterproof 'shell' are attached) will be much bulkier and take longer to dry.

Sometimes it's not possible to use cloth nappies, especially if we are heading into a damp and wet environment where drying them wouldn't be possible. On these occasions, we use disposable nappies, although we always try to reduce our impact by opting for biodegradable ones.

The downside of disposable nappies is that you must carry them out with you (even biodegradable ones). They can get very heavy when used, and after a couple of days, that's going to be a serious smelly weight you've got to lug around! You might therefore want to account for a bin stop en route.

Whatever style of nappy you choose, make sure you take plenty. On more than one occasion, I've been stuck in the wild and run out of nappies; it's pretty stressful (I had no choice but to improvise with spare bits of clothes before rushing home). Don't be tempted to simply not change a nappy, as this will lead to a grumpy baby and nappy sores.

It can be handy to have a small roll mat attached to the outside of your bag (even just a square one designed for sitting on) that you can quickly grab to use as a changing mat. They barely add any weight. If you expect rain, carrying a small, lightweight tarp can shelter you while you do nappy changes, making the job a lot more comfortable for you and the baby.

POTTY TRAINING

I actually found the early stages of potty training much more stressful to handle when it came to getting outdoors. It was easier dealing with nappies than with accidents that could end up soaking through to waterproofs or sleeping gear.

Once they've cracked it, though, it feels fantastic to say goodbye to nature nappy changes. Your pile of gear reduces (although, of course, your growing child adds to your carrying weight!).

It's important to get your child used to doing 'nature wees' while you are potty training them. For boys, this is much easier. However, girls need

⬆ Dulcie enjoying the freedom to run around

to practise going while crouching down. I've found the trick is to pull their bottom clothes down to knee level and to crouch down low. If you face opposite them crouched down, you can provide support by holding them under their arms. It's quite a skill keeping balance while also relaxing enough to do a wee ... it took me a while to master this myself when I first started getting outdoors, so be patient with your children! Another trick is to pull their clothes right down to their ankles, take their weight by holding them under their armpits and get them to put their feet up on log, boulder or even up a tree, so their legs are bent and they are in a sitting position.

If your child struggles to go in nature, then take a potty with you. There are some good fold-down travel ones on the market (we use a Potette Plus Convertible Travel Potty). However, even a regular potty isn't that heavy and usually has a handle, so you can clip it to your backpack with a carabiner.

FEEDING BABIES

If you are breastfeeding, it's super-easy to get out with your baby or toddler as you have food on tap whenever they need it. Many front-facing slings also allow you the flexibility to breastfeed on the move. For formula-fed babies, or if a partner or another adult is taking them out, then feeding will require a bit more planning. Pack pre-measured amounts of powder into a dispenser or container. You'll need a travel bottle warmer (unless your baby is happy to drink it cold) and boiled water in a vacuum flask. Take more powder and water than you think you will need in case your trip is longer than planned.

When your baby starts weaning, keep them well-fed on snacks. Be mindful that feeding them on the go will increase the risk of choking, so only give them very soft, easy-to-manage food such as bread with the crusts cut off. Food pouches are great for feeding young children outdoors; you can even get reusable pouches and make your own blends and smoothies at home.

SNACK POUCH

If you are transporting a toddler in a carrier or buggy, find a pouch that you can clip on to a handle where they can access a bag of snacks. I usually use a small dry bag or a climbing chalk bag. I'll fill it with cereal and dried fruit, allowing Rivi to snack freely without me constantly having to pass food back to her every five minutes.

TIMING

Plan your adventures to work with your baby and toddler's schedule and times in the day when they are most relaxed or sleeping. Rivi has always had a very grumpy hour that usually kicks off around 5pm. Occasionally, getting outdoors will chill her out, but usually only if we are going at her pace and letting her stop a lot. Trying to cover any distance with her during this witching hour would be my idea of hell and will not result in a positive experience for anyone.

Instead, we try to get up and out early and if we want to cover bigger distances, we work it so we are on the move during her big afternoon nap. This makes hiking much more enjoyable for all the family.

Another tricky time to be aware of is near nap time when it's too early for them to sleep as it'll mess up their routine. Being carried in a sling, buggy, bike or boat lulls them into early naps. So, a good time to take a break is just before their nap when you can boost their energy a bit with a healthy snack and some running around so they'll stay awake a bit longer.

Walking with toddlers can be challenging. Switching between them hiking and you carrying them will slowly condition them to walk longer distances

MICROADVENTURING WITH BABIES AND TODDLERS

by Samantha Fletcher

....

@my_outdoor_family

PEOPLE HAVE ALWAYS SEEMED intrigued by the outdoor pursuits my partner and I have been on. Pre-kids, we never encountered any hint of negativity around getting out there and spending so much time in the great outdoors. However, when you tell people you are pregnant and are going to start a family, the mindset of others appears to shift. All of a sudden, people who once claimed to admire your love of outdoor sports start to hint that there is no way you will be able to enjoy the same lifestyle when you have children. As if they are more knowledgeable than you about what your life will look like simply because you are bringing a baby into it.

I suppose many people can't comprehend how you would navigate adventures with small children because they lack the understanding, knowledge

and passion that surround life in the outdoors. However, the opinion that I would never be able to continue doing what I love only made me more determined to make it work.

Of course, things do change; having children is huge, and it is a journey that makes you change and grow. But different doesn't mean not possible. And you might be surprised by what you take out of it: adventuring with children has helped me appreciate things even more, adding to the joy.

TAKING OUR FIRST FAMILY ADVENTURE STEPS

Most weekends, we can be found out microadventuring in the UK with our two boys, who are now aged four and a half (Harris) and two and a half (Arran). We love all sorts of adventurous activities, from camping and hiking to skiing, paddling and climbing, and have enjoyed slowly (and patiently) introducing the boys to various disciplines from an early age.

Camping was one of the first things we did as a family when Harris was born. We always loved camping and spending time outdoors under canvas. We used to do more wild camping before the kids came along, but we soon realised that we needed to adapt our camping style to make it more comfortable for family adventures.

We bought a larger tipi-style tent and got a log burner to go inside to help keep the tent nice and warm in the evenings. We still haven't found the perfect set-up for camping with kids (if there even is a perfect set-up), but for us, the essential things to take camping are good-quality sleeping mats. We tried a range of different sleeping arrangements with the boys and ended up settling on buying a second double self-inflating mattress so we could sleep one adult and one child on each mattress.

One of our early family camping adventures, before Arran was born,

was at Waterside House Campsite in the Lake District (www.watersidefarm-campsite.co.uk) – a site that still remains one of our firm favourite family-friendly campsites. It was the end of the season, so we had pretty much the whole campsite to ourselves. We had the most idyllic pitch and stunning views down Ullswater lake from the tent door.

During our stay, we'd been on bike rides and walks from the tent. Harris had been behaving perfectly, so next, we decided to go exploring on Ullswater with the 4.9m (16ft) Canadian canoe we'd brought with us. Paddle sports hold a very special place in my heart; they're the thing that brought my partner and I together. While paddling with young children has meant changing our usual approach (my partner likes white water and dropping off the edge of waterfalls!), we've both embraced the flat waters as a family and enjoyed a more laid-back approach.

Our early attempts at paddling with Harris didn't go entirely to plan, though. It was breezy on Ullswater, making the water quite bumpy. It took what felt like two minutes for Harris to start complaining that he wanted to return to the tent. I tried to entertain him with toys and distract him with the views, and we pushed on up the lake. My efforts were doing little to shake Harris from his horrific mood. It felt like we'd been canoeing for ages, but half an hour on a boat with a screaming toddler feels like a very long time; we'd barely made any distance from the campsite!

The return to the tent was thankfully speedy, with a tailwind in our favour, and Harris perked up once back on dry land with a hot chocolate in hand. He was quite reluctant to get back in the canoe for a while after that, and we decided that we would just wait until he was a little older. We learned from the experience and now only take the boys out if the conditions are very good to ensure that they have the best experiences possible, which is especially important if they are new to a sport.

EXPANDING OUR ADVENTURES

We ended up buying a Thule Chariot trailer and started cycling with the kids when they were about nine months old. We soon found that the Chariot became the best purchase we had made, massively helping us get back outdoors with young kids. You can use it as a jogging buggy, a bike trailer and even a ski pulk. You can also get a sling system designed for transporting children aged between 1 and 10 months old and another set-up for 6- to 18-month-olds.

I was keen to get back to cycling after having my first child, and the Thule Chariot enabled us to do this, building up to bigger trips and tagalong bikes when the boys were old enough.

Climbing was another sport that I was desperate to get back to. It was probably our favourite activity before the children came along and I greatly missed it when I was pregnant. We introduced the boys to climbing at about 18 months old. I don't mean full-pitched rock climbs; rather, roped boulder scrambling to give them a basic introduction to the concept of rock climbing. It is important to allow children to take part in risk-taking activities, and as adults,

we should aim to teach our children to be more risk-aware rather than risk-avoidant. Climbing provides the perfect opportunity to discuss the risks involved when adventuring outdoors, especially when exploring large drops and exposed ground. It helps us to explain why we use ropes, the need to wear harnesses and helmets, and the importance of clear communication and listening skills.

WORTH IT IN THE END

I think the amount of organisation needed to get outside with babies and toddlers is perhaps the biggest challenge! Young children are unpredictable, so you must be prepared for any eventuality. This became considerably more true when I had my second child; having a baby in a pushchair and a toddler on foot was hard to manage at times.

We've found that illness has also often made getting outdoors difficult. When my first child started nursery, he seemed to catch all the bugs, which would scupper our plans. Then, of course, there's the challenge of the great British weather. You often hear the saying 'there is no such thing as bad weather, only unsuitable clothing' but even when kitted up in the warmest waterproofs, kids can sometimes find miserable weather a bit of a deal-breaker. We can get away with short bouts of activity in cold/wet/windy weather, but the kids make it clear when they have had enough.

Although getting outdoors poses its challenges for young families with babies and toddlers, the days when everything goes well make it completely worth it! There are always going to be days when things don't go to plan, and it feels like it is far too much effort to get outside, but these experiences just help us to learn how to deal with life outdoors with kids and how to make it easier each time we get out.

It has been very important to us that we have been able to get back out, keeping in touch with the lifestyle we had before we became parents. Heading outdoors has always been the only thing that truly helps me to clear my mind from the stress of day-to-day life. I have found that getting the kids outside helps lift their mood, too. Introducing the boys to a range of outdoor experiences so early will undoubtedly enable them to develop a lifelong love while teaching them all about the wonderful things mother nature has to offer.

Pausing after a long hike in the Lake District, UK

CONTINUING TO

ADVENTURE FOR

YOURSELF

Although this book is a guide for adventuring as a family, it was also important to have a space that acknowledges the importance of continuing to adventure for yourself. Adventuring with children, while utterly brilliant and possible, is also very different to adventuring by or for yourself: it's riddled with far more responsibility; it's more tiring – physically, mentally and emotionally; and it brings huge limitations and far fewer quiet moments.

Shortly after Rivi celebrated her second birthday, I decided to carve out some time to do an adventure for myself. I'd only left her for two nights in a row before (which at the time felt like a lot), but this would be a big jump to five nights away. Not only that, but I'd be in the Lake District, which was half a day's drive away, should I need to rush home.

To make matters worse, Rivi fell ill just a couple of days before I was due to leave. As you'd expect, she was hugely clingy to me and didn't want to leave me for a moment. I was close to quitting my adventure plans, but Gil convinced me otherwise. I'm lucky to have a very supportive partner who takes an equal share in childcare and has encouraged me from day one to continue as much as I could with the things I enjoyed before becoming a mum.

Leaving for the train station was one of the hardest things I've ever done. Seeing my subdued toddler wave me off as she snuggled into her dad made me feel like a terrible mum. I cried and then reasoned with myself: *You've made the decision now. Riddling yourself with guilt won't serve anyone. The best thing you can do is enjoy the adventure, make the most of it and come back refreshed and energised.*

←« Watching the sunset from a wild camping spot in the Lake District, UK

So that's exactly what I did. There were definitely moments (and a few more tears) where I still questioned if I was being selfish or else was worrying about Rivi. Mostly, though, I found that once I'd stepped off the train, I could switch off from mum mode and be fully present. For the next few days, I packrafted, hiked and wild camped across the Lake District with a great friend. It was challenging but so rewarding being back at an adult pace that meant I could stretch my legs, sit and look at the view on breaks, feed myself before anyone else and soak up the bliss of uninterrupted nights.

Undoubtedly, this adventure served my family as much as myself, as I returned happier, less stressed and overflowing with joy, having had some much-needed time out for myself. It's why we now regularly take turns to allow the other to go off and do their own adventures.

TAG-TEAMING OR A SUPPORT CREW

Another approach to adventuring alone while you still have children to care for is to tag-team. What this means is that you and another adult take turns doing your adventure activity – split by hours, sections or days. While one adult is adventuring, the other does childcare (as Tim Moss did with his Dales Way adventure, see page 34). This allows you to reconvene in campsites, hostels or at home in the evenings.

Alternatively, if a loved one is happy to provide support and have a little road trip, they can follow you on your adventure, meeting at pre-arranged points or at the end of each day.

Both require a supportive adult and good organisation but can provide a solution if you aren't ready or able to be away overnight from your children.

ADVENTUROUS SUMMER CAMPS

If you don't have the luxury of someone capable (or willing) to take your children for a weekend or more, residential summer camps could be a good alternative. They provide childcare and free time for you and an enjoyable experience for your child that will likely help boost their confidence.

Residential or day summer camps take children as young as seven; many are dedicated to specific outdoor activities, including sailing or surfing camps. For an all-round adventure camp, I recommend the Active Training and Education Trust, a not-for-profit that runs residential holidays – known as Superweeks (www.superweeks.co.uk). On these holidays, your children can look forward to games, walks, creativity and lots of outdoor fun. I was lucky to attend ATE Superweeks when I was younger; they were a highlight of my childhood and played a big part in instilling in me a love of the outdoors and adventure from a young age – especially as I grew up in a very un-outdoorsy family!

⚓ Finding time to still adventure for myself. Enjoying a multi-day pack-rafting adventure

MAKE CHANGES
THAT SUPPORT
ADVENTURING

Many families can reach their outdoor and adventure ambitions without making big changes. For some, though, it may feel like too many barriers are in the way. This could be a lack of money, not enough time, or simply needing to know where to start. If this is the case, it might be time to reflect on your lifestyle and recognise that changing the support or fabric of your day-to-day life could lead you to the life of adventure you desire.

⚡ ⤳ Residential summer camps, like Superweeks, are an excellent opportunity for children to have some outdoor fun while making new friends

TIME AND MONEY

Many argue that the outdoors is free, and in some senses, it is. But it's also true that it's reckless to go on adventures without suitable gear (and outdoor gear does not come cheap) and it can be costly to travel to natural spaces in the first place, especially if you live somewhere more urban.

Since leaving behind our London life to hike the Israel National Trail, Gil and I have chosen to live more frugally day-to-day – buying only second-hand items, living in a small rented home, owning just one small car, walking/using public transport as much as possible, repairing worn clothes, etc. This not only supports our mission to reduce our impact on the planet, but it also means we have considerably more funds to put towards our main love in life: adventuring and exploration.

These sacrifices also enable us to have perhaps the most valuable asset for any outdoor enthusiast: more time. We can both sustain our lives comfortably working part-time, allowing dozens of long weekends in the year to get out into the hills or camping.

Making changes can be scary, but doing so might award your family a lifestyle that allows you to prioritise the things that matter to you. This could be anything from making financial sacrifices, such as reducing present giving or skipping eating out so you can replace your leaky family tent, to making bigger structural changes, such as moving to the country, where it's cheaper, and you are closer to nature (as Sarah did with her family, see page 68).

FINDING SUPPORT THROUGH COMMUNITY

Communities are powerful things. I should know: I founded and run one of the biggest outdoor communities in the world, Love Her Wild! Communities are a great place to forge friendships, share skills, seek inspiration and motivation, and, perhaps most importantly, provide a supportive space that encourages you to take braver steps.

If you are struggling to take your first steps as a family, my biggest bit of advice is to connect with a community near you (check out the list of family-friendly adventure communities, see page 312) and to start making friends who will support you all in getting outdoors more. Another place you might find like-minded families is at one of the many family-focused outdoor festivals, such as Camp Kindling (www.campkindling.co.uk) or Gone Wild with Bear Grylls (www.gonewildfestival.com).

Alternatively, some campsites operate as family adventure centres, making them a great place to connect with others, such as the Family Camping Group (www.familycampinggroup.co.uk).

VOLUNTEERING OUTDOORS

We've all heard of groups such as Scouts, Girl Guides and the Duke of Edinburgh Award scheme, whose mission is to provide children with new friendships, skills and adventures. But adults can also benefit from becoming involved in these groups as much as children. On page 73, Nisbah Hussain shares how setting up a Scout group has led to numerous memorable outdoor adventures as a family.

These groups usually rely on volunteers, and often provide training and kit. They are usually happy to take complete beginners who are willing to learn.

Get involved:

- **Scouts:**
www.scouts.org.uk
- **Girl Guides:**
www.girlguiding.org.uk
- **Duke of Edinburgh:**
www.dofe.org
- **Army Cadets:**
www.armycadets.com

A NEW LIFE IN THE COUNTRY

by Sarah White

@explorenorthwaleswithme

I TAKE ANOTHER SIP of coffee as I sit in the sun, looking out over green rolling hills. I can hear the kids running through the wildflowers in our garden and swinging on the rope swing hanging from the large birch tree separating our home from the farmer's fields surrounding us.

As I sit, I plan our adventure for the day. A bike ride at the local trail centre? A hike up the Berwyn mountains? Or maybe a day by the lake with the paddleboard and barbecue? All of which are within easy access of our new home. I pinch myself, is this really my life now?

It is, but...

I think back to that time I sat on the floor of a tiny bedroom, a wriggly eight-month-old climbing over me as tears rolled down my face for the third time that day. I remember the never-ending shushing and swaying, hoping the door would go any minute and my husband would come and take over bedtime. Knowing full well that after his nine-hour shift at one of the busiest bike shops in the country, he too will be dreaming of slumping on the sofa and passing out.

No time for ourselves, no time for each other, no time for our new little family, no time for doing the things we love.

I knew we couldn't continue like that.

FAMILY LIFE IN MANCHESTER

At the time, I was home all day on maternity leave (and loved being with my baby but was also kinda losing my mind). Tom was working all day and only saw Rebecca for a little while in the morning or as she was going to bed, and I was due to re-start work on a part-time basis, meaning that when

Tom was at work, I was at home and vice versa, so we would have very little time together as a family.

We lived in a little terrace house on an ex-council estate in Manchester, nestled between two of the busiest motorways in the country. Despite having lived in Manchester all my life, I never felt like a city girl. Tom and I always loved the outdoors and adventure and dreamed of living somewhere that supported this lifestyle. But how could we get there? How could we create the outdoorsy, adventure-filled life we dreamt of for our family when we couldn't even get a day off together?

Honestly, I didn't have a clue; I just knew we had to do something towards making this a reality.

We started with the things we could control – our work, outgoings and free time. We managed to negotiate a job share at work, which meant we could both work part-time (so Tom could spend more time with Rebecca and share the childcare) and condensed our hours to two ten-hour days each, meaning we gained Fridays off as a family. Later, we moved to jobs we could do remotely, giving us even more flexibility.

Obviously, our income took a huge hit. So we reined in the spending, reduced our bills where we could and began to adopt a much more frugal way of life.

Slowly, we were able to introduce more adventures back into our lives. We had our camper van and long weekends on our side, so we would pack it up and hit the road every few weeks. It was a great start, but every time we visited a little rural village on our travels, we would watch the locals with envy; walking around in their outdoorsy clothes, chatting to all their friends in the little local shop, dropping their kids off at the tiny village school nestled among the wide-reaching open countryside. We knew this was the ultimate goal.

The changes in our spending, lifestyle and careers wasn't a quick process. It took several years of dreaming, hoping, planning and feeling disappointed. We added a new addition to our family in that time, and we continued talking about moving out of the city ... even settling on North Wales.

TAKING THE LEAP

A few things were holding us back from taking that final leap and moving to the countryside. We still worked part-time and didn't earn much money, so getting a mortgage on a house where we wanted was tricky. Also, we had started to build a life we loved and leaving that was scary... what if the new life we'd dreamed of turned out not to be as great as this one? It was a massive risk.

Gill Trimble, one of our favourite people in the world, was the reason we finally made the jump. Gill lived next door, but sometimes it felt like we lived together; when we had to replace the fence in the back garden we put in a low section and gate so we could easily see each other and nip into each other's houses as we pleased. We sadly received the news one day that the doctors had discovered Gill had an aggressive form of cancer and had only weeks to live.

That was it. We couldn't let life pass us by – Gill was due to retire later that year and couldn't wait to do all the fun things she had planned. She never got to do them.

We began the house hunt. We weren't having much success, so we widened our search area and up popped a project: a little white cottage with yellow shutters and a beautiful garden in a Wales/England border town. It was soon clear why it was so cheap: a housing estate was being built right next to it. My immediate reaction was 'no', but Tom poetically reminded me that it was 'on the edge of Heaven'. It had a beautiful garden and, while not as rural as we'd initially hoped, we could see the benefits of being closer to 'civilisation'. It was a compromise, but hanging on to unrealistic expectations was only going to hold us back. We put in an offer.

COUNTRY LIVING

We're in our second year of country living, the girls now aged seven and four, and I can confirm that the risk paid off.

We spent the summer of last year exploring our new area – hiking the hills that surround us, loading up our bikes and bike-packing down the nearby canal, stopping to camp overnight, chasing waterfalls or heading deeper into Snowdonia for the day, finding beautiful family-friendly adventures, yet only scratching the surface of what this area has to offer.

The 'outdoor lifestyle' we had hoped for has been easily achieved, not only in the big adventures but in the day-to-day, too. The kids cycle to school every day; Tabby joined an outdoor forest school pre-school last year; I can get out on trail runs or hikes three times a week; Tom can ride his bike from the house and be in almost traffic-free lanes within a couple of minutes; a quick walk across

a few farmers' fields leads us to the local playground; and with beautiful walks all around us, we can even fit in mid-week after-school hikes. The girls have both grown in confidence and have 'found their voice'.

Some of the things I love most about our new life are rarely included in the 'move to the country' ideals many of us have. I certainly didn't expect them. For example, the slow pace of life. This is a hard one to explain, but growing up in the city is a bit like jumping on a fast-moving roller coaster – you move and live fast. And you don't realise that you're doing it. Until, that is, you walk into a small village shop to quickly grab a loaf of bread but end up gathered around the till having a long chat. And it's the same at the tip or the pub and, basically, anywhere you go. It's such a wholesome and refreshing way to live.

The other unexpected but overwhelmingly fantastic thing to come from our move is friends. Friends who have common interests and hobbies, friends who also love to spend weekends outdoors with the kids, friends who pop over for a morning brew and leave two meals later, friends who will help out when you're sick or running late to collect the kids from school.

It's not all running through wheat fields as we live, laugh and love our new life. We've been forced to live an *even more* frugal life as we manage the necessary house renovations. The building site next door was never what we imagined, and it's taken us some time to adjust to the lack of convenience of country living.

However, I would choose this bumpy, slow country lane life over the road we were heading down in our previous city life any day. It's been the best decision we ever made for our family!

Life will never be the same again

VOLUNTEERING WITH THE SCOUTS

by Nisbah Hussain

@fiveadventurers

'Actually, the best gift you could have given her
was a lifetime of adventures.'
LEWIS CARROLL

BEING A BRITISH-ASIAN MUSLIM woman, I grew up with little exposure to the great outdoors. It felt like something my community avoided like the plague. However, this all changed in my teens while on a school trip that saw me sitting under a star-speckled sky in the Yorkshire moors. It sparked a fire in my belly and I realised I was missing out on the joys mother nature has to offer. That night, I vowed to myself to do what I could to make things better for the next generation of young people and to inspire them to connect to the outdoors.

Fast-forward two decades and I was suddenly a stay-at-home mother of little adventurers and the other half of a couple. We have been blessed with four children: Maya (aged 14), Raihan (aged 12), Zayn (aged ten) and baby Arya. Together, we are the Hussain Khalid family of six, with a real passion for

adventures in the great outdoors, both close to home and across the globe.

As a young family, we decided to make the move back to Lancashire, which seemed worlds apart from the leafy Warwickshire suburbs we had left behind. As I looked around our community, I realised not much had changed for young people who live there. So, with the support of my family, I embarked on a new adventure of volunteering by setting up the 1V Scouts. This provides opportunities for youth and the wider community, but little did I know at the beginning that it would impact our lives, changing them for the better. We are now much closer as a family and more connected to the community and feel like true outdoor adventurers. Volunteering with the Scouts has given us an opportunity to try and experience new things that we never would have had a chance of doing otherwise. It really was one of the best decisions I've ever made.

THE JOYS OF VOLUNTEERING TOGETHER

I am often asked why I set up my own Scouts group when there are so many problems associated with this, and there are already groups in existence. Our group was purely needs-led. Traditional, weekday Scout groups are not an option for young Muslims who attend extra-curricular Islamic Studies lessons. Setting up a group that met at the weekend allowed access to young people who would otherwise never have had a chance of going.

Volunteering and running this group has taken over our lives, but in a positive way. You start to see opportunities in everything you do, and plan how you can bring that to your group. Local hikes, woodlands and canals that you would otherwise overlook become potential places to explore. You find yourself away on holiday quietly adding new activities or adventures to your never-ending list of things you want to do.

When I set up the group, my little adventurers were too young to be members. However, they have each joined the group over the years, and even Doc has become a leader. Whether it's with Scouts, Guides or another similar outdoors-based organisation, volunteering as a family opens so many doors and I would wholeheartedly recommend it.

The list of what we've taken away from this opportunity as a family is endless. It includes:

- learning to be skilled and confident in the outdoors, which has helped us plan our own adventures as a family
- acquiring the kit we need to be outdoors
- having easier access to so many nature-based and adventurous activities that would be difficult to access as an individual family. As you fall into a worldwide family with the Scout organisation, the networking possibilities with like-minded individuals are endless. Examples include sleeping in hammocks or rock climbing in Wales, coasteering in the Atlantic ocean or sleeping under Dippy in the Natural History Museum
- having access to cheaper pricing when booking as a group
- being given opportunities to plan and execute large-scale trips (nationally and internationally)
- making memories together as a family. Every year, our Scouting memories are often the ones we remember the most. While it is always amazing to hear second-hand about the adventures that your children have, being there to witness them climbing to the top of the wall, learning to light a fire, overcoming other challenges and helping the younger members of the group is what will truly warm your heart.

ADVENTURES WITH THE SCOUTS

The Lake District is one of the most iconic outdoor adventure destinations in the UK. We have been lucky enough to be able to experience several group camps in this region. The Lake District will forever hold a special place in our hearts. It was the place where we first lit a campfire and sang all the campfire songs our young people had only seen others do on TV shows. It was where we first cooked, sat outdoors and drank hot chocolate by a fire, telling one another stories. It was the first place my Scouts had slept outdoors; they were in awe of how many stars there were in the dark sky. It was also the first time many of them got to try adventurous activities, from water activities on Lake Windermere to tree climbing, crate staking and ziplining.

One of the most memorable Scout adventures I have done so far, though, was our outdoor trip to Cornwall. Growing up in an area of deprivation meant that many of us had very little. This has made me more money savvy than most. I am a great believer in getting good value for money and am renowned for negotiating the maximum 'bang for my buck'. Following the impact of the pandemic, we decided to take our older Scouts and explorers for a four-day trip in Cornwall, having discovered that none of our Scouts had visited the county before.

Our base was in Par, and over the days, we managed to fit in a huge range of activities. We did coasteering, visited the Minack Theatre, had multiple campfires and barbecues, completed the via ferrata course, including ziplining across the valley, had surf lessons, explored the Eden Project and prayed Salah at sunset on Par beach.

It was an epic adventure, during which we managed to pack in so much in so little time with a limited budget, helped massively by being able to access group discounts. It showed me that even with crazy transport costs, you could undertake lots of activities and not price anyone out.

Getting outdoors with kids, especially young ones, can be daunting, but I wholeheartedly recommend it! If you are new to the outdoors or feeling apprehensive, getting involved and volunteering in a local organisation like the Scouts can make the transition much easier. It will open doors that you never knew existed, and access to the outdoors is unparalleled.

Just be aware: life will never be the same again (in the best possible way!).

CAMPING
ADVENTURES

Pitching a tent for a wild camping adventure in Dartmoor National Park, UK

OUR ADVENTURES

UNDER THE STARS

'Crap! We've forgotten the Moses basket.'

Gil dropped the masses of bags wedged under his arms and sighed, 'I'd better go back then.'

We'd only just arrived at our campsite. It was starting to feel like an epic camping adventure, and we hadn't even put a tent up yet. We'd already stopped twice leaving the drive, making a last-minute dash for forgotten items; the baby had needed the usual just-as-we're-leaving feeds and then nappy changes, and now we'd realised we had left her Moses basket (which was to be her bed for the night) on the kitchen table.

Thankfully, we'd decided to book at a campsite just ten minutes from home – a surprisingly sound decision for two such sleep-deprived first-time parents.

While Gil headed home for the Moses basket (hoping not to bump into the neighbours who'd just, half an hour previously, all been marvelling at how amazing we were camping with a young baby), I popped open a camping chair and settled in with my sleepy ten-week-old in my lap. She made some cute newborn snuffly noises before closing her eyes and falling asleep. I took a deep breath. The campsite was deadly quiet, apart from the odd rustle of leaves and birds. It was a basic site, with just a handful of pitches and a simple compost toilet. We'd picked it not just because of its proximity to home but also because the pitches were far apart, and we were conscious of the potential for night-time crying.

My mood shifted from frazzled and annoyed to grateful for the peace and gentle breeze. It had been pretty stressful getting the car packed. This hadn't been a lightweight packing experience. Newborns need a lot of stuff, including a generous amount of cloth nappies and plenty of spare clothes and then bedding, too – just in case there were leaks. And I was worried about the temperature at night. How many layers should she

⚑ Camping for the first time as a family, at a local campsite, when Rivi was ten weeks old

have on? We threw them all in. The sleeping advice online for camping with babies was minimal, to say the least, so we opted for her overnight Moses basket.

When Gil arrived (thankfully without being spotted by the neighbours), I plonked the baby into the Moses basket and we set about unloading our gear into our tent. Our two-man MSR Hubba Hubba provided just enough space for us to lie next to each other with the Moses basket at our heads. We stored the rest of our clothes and items away from the basket by our feet.

It had taken a mammoth effort to get everything packed and to fight the feeling of wanting to give up on the idea of camping with such a young baby. An echo of my old adventurous self caused me to persevere, aware that if we didn't bite the bullet now, it'd be several more months until the weather was warm enough to try again.

We may have just been ten minutes from home, but it felt like we'd landed on another planet. With no screens or chores in sight, we had no choice but to cosy up by the fire, graze on food and chat (we promised ourselves no baby chat ... that lasted about five minutes).

Rivi woke up twice in the night, less than she did at home, and we relished the chance to be outside and feel like brave, adventurous parents for a bit.

It was a huge success!

CAMPING, IN ALL VARIETIES

Camping has become a staple activity in our lives, consistently bringing us closer to the outdoors, no matter the weather. Sleeping under the stars in any capacity is the perfect way to get a break from your routine. The fact that it requires minimal physical activity and not a huge amount of planning makes it ideal for families. Cracking camping is a good place to start for any family taking their first steps into outdoor adventures!

It's also an incredibly diverse activity, and you are by no means limited to simply camping in a tent at a campsite. By the time Rivi was ten months old, we were ready to try our first wild camp. It turned out to be surprisingly easy (apart from having to transport all the gear); we didn't need to worry about being noisy, and there was loads of space for her to run around without worrying about cars or tripping over other people's guy ropes.

We've had many nights camping at festivals, making ourselves a comfortable base and using an off-road buggy to navigate the site. Keen to spread our enjoyment of camping to others, we started an annual family camp-out with local friends who have children of a similar age. We head somewhere near the beach each year so the kids can play together while the adults sit around the fire chatting in the evenings.

Since having Rivi, we've also discovered a love of glamping. Glamping is a form of camping but with accommodation and facilities that are more luxurious. It's perfect for families as it's easy and comfortable and allows you the flexibility to continue camping throughout colder months.

Rivi's introduction to glamping was quite an impressive one. We stayed overnight at the beautiful All Saints' Church in Langport, Somerset, trying out a new glamping concept called champing (church camping – www.champing. co.uk). The church was locked up for the night and we were given a

>> Champing (camping overnight in churches) makes for a great winter family adventure

key so we had access to camp overnight at the end of the pews under the looming stained-glass windows.

Stormy weather kept us from exploring the nearby nature, so instead, we cosied up in our (provided) camp beds and hot water bottles while Rivi merrily crawled up and down the pews. Occasionally, we'd have to brave the winds and rain to dash to the compost toilet at the end of the graveyard – an especially eerie experience at night. The highlight was being woken early in the morning by light shining through the stained-glass windows.

Perhaps my fondest glamping stay, though, was at Nature's Nest in the Wye Valley (www.naturesnestglamping.co.uk), where we spent a long weekend with Rivi, Dulcie and Cooper. It being late October and not feeling like braving our tent, we opted for a more comfortable safari tent. The site was set in a huge field with fire pits and wonderful views.

⬆ Camping overnight in All Saints' Church in Langport

⬇ (AND OPPOSITE TOP): Glamping in a safari tent at Nature's Nest glamping site, Wye Valley

It was the perfect combination of being close enough to nature for muddy walks, dinners around the fire, star gazing and space for the kids to roam, with the luxury of a cosy bed and warm log burner to keep us all toasty at night. The children all still talk about this trip (especially about the 'secret hidden bed' that was in the safari tent); it's a good reminder that camping and adventures don't have to involve discomfort and suffering!

Our new-found love of glamping eventually led us to buy a 4m (13ft) bell tent (for bargains, look for ex-display models or buy out of season). While not the cheapest of purchases, you don't have to stay in it for many nights to justify the price compared to the cost of glamping. It's a very heavy bit of kit – only suitable if you're camping near your car – and requires space to dry properly after use, but it's easy to assemble and put down and incredibly spacious.

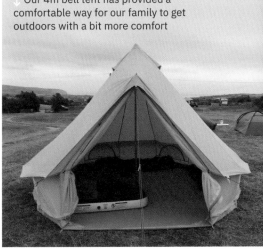

Our 4m bell tent has provided a comfortable way for our family to get outdoors with a bit more comfort

Whatever your camping of choice – tent, glamping, rooftop tent or camper van – have your gear organised into boxes at home (one for sleeping gear, another for food/stove items, etc). This will save you a lot of time when the weather changes or you feel an urge to get away. You simply throw your boxes into the boot and head off to enjoy your adventure under the stars...

FAMILY CAMPING
PACKING LIST

Your family camping packing list will vary depending on your camping style. If you're attempting a wild camp, you will need to pack light. One of the easiest ways to reduce the gear you need is to cut out the stove and take only cold food. I'd only attempt this for an overnight trip and not if you're expecting cold temperatures.

If you have the luxury of a car nearby, you can throw in a few 'optional extras' to make the experience much more comfortable. Off-road buggies or pack-down trolleys are great bits of kit for transferring all your gear if your pitch is a bit of a walk from the car.

⚐ All the kit we packed for a wild camping adventure

THE BASICS

SLEEPING

- tent
- sleeping bags
- roll mats
- spare blanket

ACCESSORIES

- torches
- extra batteries
- phone and battery pack (in a dry bag)
- pocket knife

PERSONAL

- clothes and shoes
- waterproofs
- warm layers
- beanies/woolly hats
- sun hats and sunglasses
- sunscreen
- insect repellent
- toothbrushes and toothpaste
- soap bar
- comb
- quick-dry towel
- first aid kit and any medication

COOKING

- stove and gas
- pot/pan
- matches
- plates and/or bowls
- cutlery
- mugs
- sponge and washing-up liquid
- tea/coffee
- food and snacks
- water bottles

IF TAKING AN INFANT

- portable cot/Moses basket
- nappies
- comforter
- compostable baby wipes
- compostable nappy bags

OPTIONAL EXTRAS

- camping chairs
- folding table
- pillows
- ball
- cards
- swimming gear
- books
- dustpan and brush (for cleaning the tent)
- mallet
- additional blankets

Top tips for keeping costs down

Kitting out the family with outdoor gear can be expensive. As much as possible, I try to get items second-hand from places like Marketplace, eBay and Vinted. Or I borrow from friends (while making it abundantly clear that I'm equally happy to share what I have too). There are also organisations like Kitsquad (www.kitsquad.co.uk), which can support low-income families with free outdoor gear.

Top tips for family camping gear

• **Buy a tent that is fit for your long-term purpose.** If you intend to backpack carrying it, then you will need to prioritise weight (like our MSR Elixir 4 tent). A more spacious tent might be a better choice if you will always be camping near to your car.

• **Note that a four-person tent can only just squeeze in four people** sleeping without much additional space for any bags. So a five-person tent would be more comfortable if you are a family of four. A family of three would ideally use a four-person tent.

• **If you have a bed wetter, avoid down or cotton materials.** Sleep them in a synthetic sleeping bag, which can dry quickly during the day if it's hung out in the sun or a warm place.

• **Do a practice run** with all your gear before going camping. Set up the tent in your living room or garden and spend all night sleeping in it. If you have problems or punctures, it's better to discover this at home when you can transfer to your beds in the middle of the night. If you don't have space for this, your children can sleep on their mats and sleeping bags on the floor for a night to get them used to them.

• **We've always taken at least a few small picture books** on every adventure. I've found it the easiest way to calm children down before bed. Alongside the books, I tell them stories, often just something from my past, like how I met my husband, the best holiday I ever had or the day they were born. It always amazes me how much they enjoy listening to these true accounts.

SAFE SLEEPING
WHEN CAMPING WITH
CHILDREN

Following the same guidelines you use at home when camping with children is essential to keep them comfortable and safe. This is especially true for infants who are at higher risk of overheating or exposure. The reality of this is that camping with an infant can be limiting as you'll need to take a travel cot or Moses basket suitable for overnight sleeping.

You can use the below as a rough guideline but please check the most up-to-date information on safe sleeping. Note that this is based on the average sizes of children in each age bracket, and healthy children without additional needs. If you are unsure or have a child with health conditions, you should consult a medical professional for guidance.

≫→ Rivi's introduction to camping, aged ten weeks

⌐⊦ Campsites that allow you to drive up to your pitch mean you can pack as much kit as you can fit in the car!

SLEEPING REQUIREMENTS FOR CHILDREN

Age	Sleeping in	Sleeping on	Sleeping under	Note
Up to one year	The infant should wear a sleepsuit with an extra thin layer (like a short-sleeved bodysuit) underneath if it's cold. Wool sleepsuits will be the most effective at keeping them warm in cold weather. They should then sleep in an infant sleeping bag. There are different rated togs (eg 1.5, 2, 3.5) and the thickness you choose to use will depend on the weather and how warm your baby gets at night. Do not put a hat or hood on an infant as this can cause them to overheat.	A travel cot, a Moses basket or a nest approved for independent overnight sleeping (such as a Purflo Sleep Tight Baby Bed). There are pop-up or travel cots available, which are probably the most lightweight option on the market. Infants should sleep feet to foot, always on their back, in a clear, flat sleeping space on a firm, flat waterproof mattress.	If you use an additional blanket it should be light and breathable and fully tucked in. Remember a blanket folded in half provides twice the insulation.	If you're unsure – use fewer layers. Babies are at a higher risk of overheating than getting cold. Check a baby's temperature by feeling the back of their neck and/or chest. If it's clammy or sweaty remove a layer (their hands and feet will always feel cold to the touch). The ideal sleeping temperature for babies is 16–20ºC (61–68ºF). If you are worried in the night that your baby is too cold, the quickest way to warm them up is to give them a cuddle against your skin.
One to two years	Pyjamas or base layers, with an extra layer (ie a vest top) in colder weather. Avoid cotton. Many toddler travel beds have built-in sleeping bags. If not then put them in an infant sleeping bag – most brands go up to three years old.	Toddler camping beds should have a guard to keep them secure and warm at night. A travel cot, toddler air bed (like a Snuggle Pod) or a roll-out bed (like a My First ReadyBed) is ideal.	If your toddler needs it, add a light, breathable blanket once the temperature has dropped.	It's not safe to put a toddler in a large sleeping bag that is designed for an older child or adult.

Age	Sleeping in	Sleeping on	Sleeping under	Note
Three to six years	Pyjamas or base layers, with an extra layer (ie a vest top) in colder weather. Avoid cotton. There are lots of children's sleeping bags available for ages three-plus. Pick one that's suitable for the weather you intend to camp in.	Your child is now old enough to sleep on a roll mat. There are lightweight inflatable camping roll mats available for children, although a foam one is cheaper and might be less slippery. If they move around a lot at night, you may still wish to give them something with sides. There are roll beds (like Junior ReadyBed) and regular children air beds available with or without sides. Another option is to use a raised fold-out camp bed.	If your child needs it, add a light, breathable blanket once the temperature has dropped.	If you're using a foam roll mat, buy a three-quarter length one to save you carrying extra weight, or get a foldable one that you can fold in half to add extra insulation.
Seven-plus years	Pyjamas or base layers, with an extra layer (ie a vest top) in colder weather. Avoid cotton. It is safe for a child to now sleep in an adult-sized sleeping bag, although be aware that they won't be as effective at keeping them warm if there is lots of additional space inside. A child's sleeping bag will be narrower and will provide them with better insulation.	Sleep your child on a camping foam roll mat or inflating mat. If weight and size aren't an issue, you could use an inflatable bed or futon.	Fleece blankets can make effective extra warm layers if needed.	If your child has a tendency to get tangled up in a sleeping bag intended for an adult, use a zip lock tie to tighten the foot of the sleeping bag to make it shorter in length.

CAMPING, BOTHY AND BIVVY ADVENTURES

by Kerry-Anne Martin

....

@twoweeadventurers

IT WAS REALLY ONLY through becoming a parent that I came to prioritise adventure in my own life. Although on reflection I recognise that I'd always loved spending time outdoors, camping and hillwalking weren't part of my childhood upbringing. They were something I discovered an enjoyment for as an adult and, later, as a parent. With a husband working long, inconsistent hours and no family living locally to assist with childcare, I quickly realised that if I wanted outdoor adventures to play a part in my life, I had no choice but to involve my son (Finn, aged 12) from his earliest days and to do so exclusively, often adventuring as a solo mum and child.

What I didn't realise at first is that adventuring with children can help us as adults pause to see the beauty and wonder of what's right before us, which might otherwise have been missed. On one of our early bivvy adventures to a remote upland loch, a 9.6km (6-mile) walk took us a challenging five hours after a path shown on the map failed to materialise. At 8pm, we finally arrived at the perfect patch of white granite sand fringing a serene blue-green loch just as the sun set below the distant mountains. I was tired, hungry, mentally exhausted and intent upon hastily unpacking the stove to make a late supper.

I was stopped in my tracks though by my five-year-old dancing up and down the beach with a look of pure rapture on his face. He was singing over and over to himself, 'I love today, I love today, today is the best day of my life'. It caused me to pause, take in the beauty and change my perceptions on how I thought the day had gone.

NOT ALL GOES TO PLAN

Our adventuring life together didn't start in the most auspicious way. Finn's introduction to camping,

aged six months, was at a campsite in north-west Scotland as a family. On the journey, I started to feel ill and spent the weekend in an exhausted stupor shuttling between the tent to breastfeed and the toilet blocks to throw up. After returning home, selective amnesia obviously kicked in (a common feature of our adventures!) as I gushed to others about how much fun it had been camping with a little one.

The following summer, unperturbed, we returned to camp in a field in the north of Scotland. We had not long snuggled down for the night when Finn woke us up with a truly spectacular vomiting extravaganza. No sooner had we mopped up as best we could with any spare clothes than we were promptly treated to an encore. His sleeping bag, the tent walls and just about everything else were covered. A few months later, seemingly not put off and with Finn not quite two years old, I had a fit of misguided enthusiasm, deciding I was ready for our first camping trip as a solo parent.

On our first night, we pitched up at the campsite in Ullapool, ready to take the early morning ferry to the Outer Hebrides. Having taken two days to get to our final destination on the sublime west coast of the Isle of Lewis, I lasted all of a night. I was mentally and physically exhausted (Finn had always been an unsettled baby and was still waking every two or three hours through the night) and admitted to myself that I couldn't cope. I therefore made the long and not-as-hasty-as-I'd-have-liked retreat home.

THE FIVE BOTHY CHALLENGE

As Finn turned four and was capable of walking longer distances, I began to widen our adventuring boundaries a little. We continued with regular nature walks, night walks, all-weather picnics and annual car-camping trips but also went camping using public transport and slept out on a local hill under the stars in bivvy bags (thin, light, waterproof outer bags that go around your sleeping bag and serve as a simple shelter).

Finn also spent his first night in a bothy – a basic shelter, often in remote locations, that is open (and free) to all. They usually come with no running water, toilet or facilities. After that first bothy experience, I had a flash of inspiration (and obviously more selective amnesia!) and sent a proposal to The Next Challenge Expedition Grant (www.thenextchallenge.org/grant/), an annual grant run by adventurer Tim Moss, to 'spend five nights in five bothies within five weeks with a five-year-old'.

After a couple of months without hearing anything, I had easily convinced myself I'd been unsuccessful and gave a sigh of relief as time had brought with it the stark realisation of what such an adventure would entail. When I finally received the news that my application had been successful, I was a) too embarrassed and b) too stubborn to back out. So, we spent a month that October travelling between bothies in Galloway, the Isle of Skye and Torridon.

Despite being woken by a horde of mice the first night, a rising wind repeatedly banging the door the second night, and the night-time goings on of some interesting bothy characters the third night (not to mention Finn emphatically declaring after bothy number four that he never wanted to spend another night in a bothy ever again!) we did achieve our goal. I still look back on our bothy challenge as one of our greatest, most successful adventures, although I've never since wished to repeat the experience!

ONE-YEAR BIVVY CHALLENGE

Around the same time as our bothies trip, I discovered Alastair Humphrey's (www.alastairhumphreys.com) concept of microadventures. Inspired, I decided our next challenge would be, starting in January, to sleep out (without a tent) one night every month over the whole year.

In the first month, we spent a chilly night in the back garden, keeping warm by using two sleeping bags each and hot water bottles. The first challenge was trying to assist Finn (then aged six) and then manoeuvre myself into my sleeping and bivvy bags while barely being able to move because I was dressed in so many layers of clothing. A good 15 minutes and what felt like a strenuous workout later, the second challenge was to do it all over again after Finn announced that he needed help to get out to use the toilet.

We finally fell into slumber, accompanied by a couple of tawny owls hooting in a nearby copse and the lingering scent of wood smoke. Three times during the night I had to rescue a distressed Finn who had managed to cocoon himself so effectively within his sleeping bag that he couldn't find his way out again.

It was only when I emerged from my bivvy bag to rescue him the third time that I realised it had been snowing and that a sprinkle of the white stuff had already dusted the garden and its sleeping occupants. We awoke to the light slowly returning over a Narnia-like landscape and a skein of pink-footed geese honking directly overhead.

We failed to complete our challenge in either November or December that year. Still, we did share several wonderful new experiences together, including bivvying in snow (twice!), in forests, on a beach and 700m (2,300ft) high on the summits of some of our local hills.

PLANNING FOR IT NOT TO GO TO PLAN

We continued to set ourselves outdoor-related challenges, from walking the length of the Isle of Harris for our John Muir Trust Family Award, holding a New Year snow picnic complete with candles and crackers, walking 400km (250 miles) over 40 days of Lent, Saturday night cookouts over an outdoor fire every week through the first lockdown. And backpacking and wild camping the Arran Coastal Path.

Every time we survived a new adventure, it gave me renewed courage and confidence to continue. Yet, after nearly 12 years of adventuring with my son, I'm pretty sure we've never had an adventure go smoothly and to plan! Sometimes I questioned what I was doing, like on a bitterly cold March day high in the Lakeland fells when my seven-year-old had had enough and screamed his heart out at me, point blank refusing ever to go walking again. (A couple of hours and a snack later, all the while thinking that I'd really blown it this time and that our relationship would never be the same again, that same seven-year-old turned to me and joyously exclaimed what a wonderful day he'd had!)

Sometimes, we just had to give up and bail out, like when we had a tent pole snap and collapse on us in a freak gust of wind while wild camping several miles from the nearest road. And sometimes, it just all felt too hard, like when I took a five-year-old Finn camping in the Orkney Islands by public transport, and I cried every night for three days from the sheer effort of it all. That's OK because family adventures aren't easy and are even more challenging (but conversely perhaps even more rewarding) as a solo parent when every little task takes longer. You alone are responsible for carrying everything, putting up the tent, setting up camp, fetching water and cooking, while simultaneously keeping an eye on that toddler who's about to upset the camp stove, all in torrential rain, blustery winds or a madness-inducing cloud of Scottish midges. No wonder it feels like an achievement just leaving the house!

Sometimes the best you can do is keep an open mind, stay flexible, be prepared to let go of some expectations and remind yourself repeatedly why you're doing it. Even if you don't complete what you intended to do, if at the end of the day you arrive home again safely, then it counts as a successful adventure.

It's the most challenging moments that make the best stories. Memories become a shared narrative that you'll be reminding each other of and laughing about for years to come. For all the tears, the tantrums, the feeling of being unprepared and under-qualified, the exhaustion and the mishaps, there has been pure joy, gratitude and wonder. We've both grown as individuals – developing self-confidence, self-reliance and awareness of our own limits, learning to evaluate risk, facing fears (unidentified noises in a remote bothy in the middle of the night!) and building a skill set to draw on when we face fresh challenges in our lives.

What's more, we've deepened our relationship with each other. The simple nature of camping and hiking allows for time and space to share heartfelt conversations, thoughts and feelings, free of the distractions that dominate our modern fast-paced culture. Our outdoor adventures have become normalised as a beloved part of family life and a ritual through which my son and I celebrate each other and our relationship together.

As Finn rapidly approaches his teenage years and I witness his love of adventure continue to blossom, I have more gratitude than ever for the memories and traditions we've created. The journey has been tough at times but at the end of the day, I don't believe I've ever returned from an adventure having regretted starting out!

WILD CAMPING

Wild camping is my favourite outdoor pursuit, and it's a wonderful thing to introduce your children to. The sense of quiet, being fully immersed in nature and the thrill of seeing the stars at night, miles from others, is hard to replicate.

Wild camping is legal in Scotland but illegal in England, Wales and Northern Ireland without the landowner's permission. In Scotland, if you are respectful, leave no trace and follow the protocols of wild camping, then it is generally tolerated in National Parks, along long-distance trails and in remote places.

The most important thing when wild camping is to respect nature and always to follow correct camping etiquette.

Trying camping for the first time as a family. Picking a local campsite took the stress and worry out of the trip

Wild camping etiquette

• **Don't camp if the land is obviously private,** there are houses/ farms within sight or if you need to jump a fence (unless you ask permission first).
• **Be quiet and respectful.**
• **Pitch late and leave early** and never stay more than one night.
• **Pick a spot** that requires the least amount of disruption (ie moving rocks and stones) and avoid trampling on flowers or plants.
• **Take away all your litter.**
• **Don't ever light fires;** use a camping stove if you decide to cook.
• **Never wash in the streams,** rivers, lakes or the ocean with soaps (even biodegradable and natural products change the ecosystem).
• **When going to the toilet,** be at least 50m (164ft) away from any nearby water source and dig a hole at least 15cm (6in) deep; anything that is not human waste should be taken away with you (bring decomposition nappy bags for carrying used items). Cover the hole properly when you're finished.

⚓ Views from our tent in Dartmoor National Park, UK

WILD CAMPING WITH CHILDREN

The lack of toilet facilities and running water is likely to be considered when taking children wild camping. While most children won't complain about skipping a wash, having clean water for drinking, hand washing and teeth brushing is going to take a bit of planning.

Not all children will be comfortable going to the toilet outdoors, so ensure you have practised this on nearby nature walks (following the correct protocols) first.

⚡ Rivi watching the wild horses in Dartmoor National Park

➤➤ Fires when wild camping are not permitted, but many campsites allow you to use fire pits

Not having the comfort of a car nearby also means you will need to work out how to carry your gear. Opt for more lightweight camping gear and take just the bare minimum (see page 87). This also means that your 'bail out' or 'plan B' at night is going to be tricker. For this reason, I'd suggest building up to wild camping with garden or car camping trips first.

NEARLY WILD CAMPING

If the logistics or gear is proving too difficult, or you are feeling anxious about being moved on in the middle of the night, then using Nearly Wild Camping (www.nearlywildcamping.org) could be a good alternative.

Nearly Wild Camping lists more than 200 campsites across the UK. The sites tend to be very basic – just with a tap and toilet – and usually small, giving you the same sense of quiet and back-to-basics you get from wild camping. Pitches tend to be more affordable than a regular campsite.

Nearly Wild Camping is also a great option for groups of families looking to hire an exclusive site.

KEEPING THE FAMILY
WARM WHILE CAMPING

There is nothing more miserable than not being warm enough when camping. It leads to an uncomfortable and restless night and is the quickest way to deter your children from ever wanting to go camping again! Use these top tips to keep everyone warm when camping, no matter the weather.

KEEP EVERYTHING DRY

Your camping gear and clothes won't be effective if they get wet. It's essential, therefore, that you prioritise keeping all your gear dry. Don't let children bring drinking bottles near the beds; if you put the tent up in the rain, put the outer up first to provide shelter before unloading any other gear.

THINK ABOUT WHAT EVERYONE IS SLEEPING ON

You lose lots of heat through the ground when camping. If someone gets cold, it can be more effective to add an extra layer (like a blanket or waterproof) underneath rather than over the top.

Air beds can be especially cold to sleep on (camping-specific inflatable mats usually have insulation in them, but the sort of air beds you'd use at home don't). I find even on a hot summer night, I wake up cold if I'm using an air bed. I prevent this by adding an insulating layer, usually a thick fleece blanket, between me and the bed.

NEVER GET INTO BED COLD

If you get into your sleeping bag cold, you will stay that way as you need warmth for the layers and insulation to be effective. Before sleeping, check that your children aren't feeling cold. If they are, go for a brisk walk, do some star jumps or play a game that involves running around.

If one of them wakes up cold at night, the quickest way to warm them (and you!) up is to cuddle up in the same sleeping bag. Your shared body heat will soon have you both toasty warm.

TAKE YOUR CLOTHES OFF BEFORE BED

It can be tempting for everyone to get into their sleeping bag with all their layers on. As your clothes store sweat from your body, this isn't an effective way of staying warm and might actually leave you feeling colder. Strip down, so you are only wearing your pyjamas/base layers, and give your sleeping bags a chance to warm up.

«‹ »› Children love the freedom of camping or glamping. We always prefer car-free sites, so we don't have to worry about them roaming

↑ A layering system is a great way to regulate infants' temperatures when camping

I always save a thick, clean pair of socks that I only put on before bed. I can't sleep with cold feet and find my daughter is the same!

Have spare fleeces nearby so if you feel that you or any of the family need it in the middle of the night, you can easily add a layer.

DON'T HOLD IN WEE

Having a full bladder can leave you feeling colder. Make sure you and the children go to the toilet right before bed. And make sure that they tell you if they need to go in the night, so they don't try to hold it in.

KEEP YOUR NEXT DAY'S CLOTHES TOASTY

Store your and your children's next day's clothes (just the layers you'll have against your skin) at the bottom of your sleeping bag. This will warm them up overnight, making it easier to get everyone changed the next day if it's a chilly start.

CAMPER VAN
ADVENTURES

Camper vans (or motorhomes) provide an easy, self-sufficient way to travel with children. There's a huge network of motor-friendly campsites across the UK and further afield into Europe, providing endless routes to explore.

Camper van adventures are ideal for families, providing a home-on-wheels carrying everything you need while also sheltering you from the elements better than canvas can.

⚑ Camper vans are a great way to get out on adventures as a family

⇡⇣ Enjoying a south-west road trip in our Bailey of Bristol Motorhome. Motorhomes provide a more luxurious and spacious option if a camper van feels too small for your family

Top tips for camper-vanning with kids

• **When planning a route, be realistic** about journey times and the distances your children can comfortably travel. Plenty of rest and downtime will make for a more relaxing journey.

• **Packing space is limited, so be organised** and make an effort to put things back in the same place, so they are easy to find.

• **Allocate a space for your children to fill** with toys or activities they'd like to bring along for the ride.

• **Involve your children** in route planning and setting up camp each night.

• **Blackout blinds are essential** in summer to prevent your children from thinking 5am is a reasonable wake-up time! (Of course, this might be irrelevant if you have an early rising infant anyway.)

• **Make sure your children are all seated** in correctly fitting car seats. If you plan to sleep them in a roof compartment, install a child safety net to prevent them from falling down the entrance gap at night.

• **Outdoor sheltered space** will make your journey a lot more comfortable – such as an awning or a pop-up tent that will allow you to cook outside even if it's raining.

• **If you're taking a toddler or baby,** a large outdoor storage bucket makes a great bath and a place to store all their essential items (nappies, wipes, toys, etc) when not in use.

Opening our eyes to our country's heritage and beauty

ROOFTOP TENT ADVENTURES

by Laura Bridger

@little.adventures.uk

MY AMBITION TO BEGIN our camping adventures started during the first lockdown, although it only became a reality later that year. The pandemic was a very lonely and isolating experience, being a single parent to my eight-year-old daughter while juggling work, home schooling and university. I needed a means of escape and to be free. We'd never been camping before, but it was our best option for getting away at the time. Searching for a suitable tent was a minefield, not just because of the vast number of options available but also because I needed to make sure I could erect this tent single-handedly. I soon realised that in addition to a tent, I also needed all the camping accessories that came along with it: sleeping bags, pillows, camping beds … the list goes on. How would I fit all of this in my car comfortably, as well as having enough room for my daughter and me, plus our clothes and food?

Then, I came across rooftop tents. What a revelation!

CAMPING ADVENTURES

Our bed could securely fit on top of the car and serve as storage for all our bedding and the telescopic ladder. Did I mention it also has a memory foam mattress? I took the plunge and made the order (settling on a TentBox Classic).

Since it was installed two years ago, my daughter and I have travelled all over the United Kingdom, meeting lots of lovely people and making wonderful, lifelong memories.

OUR FIRST CAMPING ADVENTURES

Our first camping trip was to a fantastic site in South Wales. We navigated our way up a steep hill to the top field of the farm. The views were spectacular. We had sheep freely roaming around us, and no roads were in sight. The perks of having a rooftop tent meant we could set up our base in just two minutes, much to the amazement of other campers. We befriended a nice neighbouring family, talking all night while toasting marshmallows around the roaring campfire. This was when I fell in love with camping – being out in nature, under the stars, without worrying about work, bills and morning alarms.

While we were in Wales, we explored the local area and stumbled across some beautiful castles and stunning nature walks; we swung on rope swings,

discovered caves and climbed waterfalls. From here, our adventures escalated, and we found a passion for hiking. While driving through Wales, my daughter noticed people climbing up a large hill and immediately took a fancy to joining in the fun. Little did we know that this wasn't just a standard hill – it was the highest peak in South Wales! We pulled up, armed with a rucksack full of water and snacks, and started our very slow ascent up to the summit. After stopping for multiple snack breaks, reaching the summit of both Corn Du and Pen y Fan felt exhilarating. After making our descent (a lot faster than our ascent), we drove back to a nearby campsite to watch the glowing orange sunset while warming up by the fire and enjoying some hot chocolate and a biscuit.

Later the same year, we decided to tackle Snowdon. My daughter was just six years old, so I had decided to book the train three-quarters of the way up, finish the walk up to the summit and then walk the descent. I thought that alone would be an accomplishment as we were beginners to hiking. However, after we arrived, my daughter decided she didn't want to take the train; she wanted to walk all the way to the top. I was shocked. We had come prepared, but I wasn't sure if I'd make it up and down myself, let alone her. Somehow, she convinced me to cancel our train tickets, and we gathered our supplies for our long hike up the mountain.

There were times when I didn't think we would make it, especially as parts of the path were incredibly steep and slippery. However, we both reached the summit thanks to lots of determination. We felt on top of the world, standing there above the clouds – the highest people at that instant in England and Wales. What a proud moment.

I had booked a lovely little campsite at the foot of Snowdon, and we spent the next few days exploring Llanberis, a beautiful small town I'd highly recommend visiting. We visited the National Slate Museum, where we discovered the history of the Welsh slate industry and how the workers lived. We also travelled slightly further afield to Sygun Copper Mine to immerse ourselves in the life of a Victorian copper miner. We walked through cold,

wet underground tunnels and large chambers, learning about stalactite and stalagmite formations. Camping has opened our eyes to Britain's heritage, and I am so grateful for that.

THE PERKS OF ROOFTOP CAMPING

For our biggest adventure yet, we organised a road trip through the Peak District up to the Lake District and then on to Scotland. We had ten whole days of adventure planned, which was made possible by having the flexibility of a rooftop tent. We weren't tied to one campsite, so we could move around freely without any hassle.

During this road trip, we explored two caves, one castle, kayaked on Loch Lomond and completed many wonderful hikes, including Kinder Scout, Black Hill and Mam Tor. The highlight of this trip was summiting Ben Nevis, the tallest mountain in the UK. At just seven years old, my daughter climbed 1,345m (4,413ft) carrying her own supplies. I am beyond proud of her courage and determination. It wasn't easy, but she kept us motivated, telling us stories and playing games. Once we had completed our descent, we got into our pyjamas, climbed up into our rooftop tent and watched a movie while eating popcorn.

One of the biggest perks of having a rooftop tent, aside from the fast set-up time and not needing to worry about packing away a large, wet tent and all the equipment inside, is all the additional storage space you gain inside your vehicle. It has taken me a while to achieve the perfect packing routine, but I think I have finally mastered it. We have storage drawers always stocked with all the necessary kit, such as cooking equipment, utensils, personal care products and long-life foods. These fit comfortably in the boot of my car and enable us to cook meals while travelling around on our adventures. Additional items such as walking poles and boots, water, extra blankets, and battery packs fit easily underneath. This set-up enables us to pack the car quickly when we want to get away for a weekend.

Investing in our rooftop tent has enabled us to see the UK and pursue the outdoors more than we could ever have imagined was possible. It's given us the freedom to explore different areas on a limited budget without spending hours stressing over logistics and packing. With it taking just two minutes to set up and five minutes to pack away, we can easily be on the move, exploring our country's history and seeing all the beauty it has to offer.

Hiking in the Brecon Beacons
National Park, Wales

TRAIL AND

MOUNTAIN

ADVENTURES

OUR ADVENTURES

ON FOOT

This suddenly seemed like a terrible idea. I was stressed about logistics and wondered if the route we had picked would be doable with a buggy. The dreaded pre-adventure-packing-for-a-family had taken us ages, and our 'to-take' pile was growing by the minute. Mostly though, I was just really tired. Packing for a big adventure with Gil was fine when both of us were on hand but Gil was currently doing the dinner-bath-bed routine with (a very grumpy and teething) Rivi, leaving me to try to work out the

⸙ ≫→ We love our Out'n'About off-road buggy. It allows us to carry more kit which means we can go longer when hiking and camping

number of snacks required to keep a baby happy, how many spare baby clothes we needed and whether Charlie Bear was an essential item or not!

This was our first multi-day adventure as a family. Rivi was 11 months old, and we had a long weekend booked off work. Our original plan had been to walk the west half of the Ridgeway. Public transport (or lack thereof) was making it tricky logistically, so we needed an alternative route. A few days before leaving, I searched online and found a mountain bike trail in Dartmoor. Traffic-free and suitable for bikes; I figured, in theory, it would also be doable with an off-road buggy.

The biggest challenge with doing a multi-day trip in Dartmoor was a lack of running water sources, meaning we'd have to carry lots of drinking water with us. I was happy we'd opted to use the off-road buggy rather than trying to carry Rivi and all the camping gear, as it would greatly help us spread the weight. After Rivi was asleep, we experimented with attaching all our gear to the buggy. Using bungee cords, most of the items fitted under the foot stand (the soft roll mats went on the seat with Rivi sitting on top). The remaining items fitted into two rucksacks, one of which we would clip to the handlebars of the buggy, the other one of us would carry.

It was a bit haphazard, but it fitted. I reasoned that if it didn't work, we'd just pack down and drive home. There was nothing to lose!

GETTING BACK TO HIKING
AS A MUM

Hiking was my saviour during my maternity leave. Going on walks often felt like my only link to my old life. I didn't find it easy picking up hiking again postpartum, though. I may have hiked a 1,000km (160-mile) trail and led teams of adults across deserts and mountain ranges but being responsible for an unpredictable, demanding baby in the wild petrified me. On top of this, my fitness had taken a big hit during pregnancy; even a short distance would leave me feeling achy and out of breath.

My first walks were as easy as you could get – walking with the buggy into town or around the local park. I then began to rely on the sling more, enjoying the fact that it enabled me to get into more of a stride and over rockier terrain. It took me a while to build up confidence, but I eventually started to go on loop walks in nature, usually about an hour in length.

A fabric sling is a great way to carry a young infant on walks

In time, the fear I had around Rivi kicking off mid-hike disappeared. If this happened, I learned that the best thing to do was to find a log, take her out of the sling and give her a feed or a tickle or just some space to change her mood. I'd then set off again, although always with the acceptance that another break might be necessary … patience is essential.

One of the styles of hikes that I enjoy most is night walking, especially in winter when the days are so short and the evenings feel so long. Being out in the dark with Rivi or my niece and nephew instantly calms them down. They love having a head torch, although I always find time to stand still, turn off the lights and listen to the night's sounds.

Of course, there were many disastrous hikes. For instance,

once when I was 20 minutes into a walk, a sudden downpour hit us. I quickly wrapped Rivi and myself in waterproofs, but she was not happy and kept pulling her hood off, leaving her drenched in minutes. She screamed her little head off as I walked/ran back to the car, feeling like a terrible mum. I sobbed in the car while feeding her breadsticks (she was now happy and babbling) before driving home.

My biggest learning in the process (and maybe with all my parenting?!) was that I wished I'd been kinder to myself. Been a bit more OK with taking things slow and trusting that in time, things get easier, my fitness would increase and I'd return to bigger and more challenging hikes.

The trails and mountains aren't going anywhere!

DAY TWO IN DARTMOOR

I opened the zip of our tent door, and Rivi squealed in excitement – ponies surrounded us! Usually, on a long-distance hike, we pack down quickly and head out early. With a baby in tow, though, it's a different pace. We decided to hang about for a couple of hours until she'd had her first nap. I thought I'd be agitated not getting going, but in fact I loved having the time to enjoy the stillness in nature, the reading time and watching the Dartmoor ponies peering at us with curiosity.

Our first day in Dartmoor – where wild camping is allowed in some areas – had been brilliant. Our Out'n'About Sport buggy worked well with all our gear and was very manageable to push along the gravel and grassy tracks

←« ↑ Wild camping and horses in Dartmoor National Park, UK

(although it took a bit more effort on any inclines). As soon as we'd left our car, which we had parked in Princetown, we'd turned down a trail behind a church and instantly found ourselves in the wilds of Dartmoor. Wide open spaces as far as you could see.

We'd had to stop for a nappy change and feed within five minutes, but I didn't care. This was the first proper adventure I'd had in almost two years, and I was bouncing with excitement! In the madness of planning, I'd forgotten to look forward to the adventure, the wild camping and tackling a trail – all things I love.

An angry cow had meant we'd needed to ditch our plan to camp near King's Tor. The great thing about wild camping is you have complete flexibility, so we'd simply taken a different path until we'd found a sheltered, flat space with a good view.

I don't think I'd ever seen a baby as excited as Rivi when we'd put up the tent. She was rolling about on the inflatable roll mats and sleeping bags, jumping and throwing herself from one side of the tent to the other. Who needs soft-play when you have a tent? Not surprisingly, it was a late bedtime by the time we got Rivi into a calm enough state for sleep.

After packing down the tent mid-morning, we were ready to tackle the 10km (6.2 miles) until our next intended wild camp spot. Rivi was still teething so it was a frustrating hike with lots of stops. I was thankful I'd brought the sling as she was much happier strapped to me while Gil pushed the buggy loaded with all our gear.

We reached Burrator Reservoir, which was as stunning as I'd hoped it would be. We knew wild camping was limited in the area, but this was even more the case with the buggy. It started to get dark, and we were all pining for some warm food. In the end, we decided to hide the buggy in some shrubbery. Carrying Rivi in a sling on my front and our gear, we stomped halfway up a steep tor where there was a convenient ledge. It was an exhausting and sweaty climb, but the view was worth it. The

⟨ Wild camping with children is great as you don't need to worry about noise or disturbing other campers

best part was that Rivi crashed with no resistance, leaving me and Gil to sit outside the tent watching the sunset over the reservoir.

A moment that dreams are made of!

ALL NEW PARENTS NEED AN ADVENTURE

With much less space for Rivi to safely crawl around, we packed down our tent and gear early the next day. Finding our buggy right where we'd left it was a relief!

It was another challenging day of hiking, but for an altogether different reason. Rivi had mellowed out, but the path underfoot became rockier and steeper. In some sections, it took Gil pushing the buggy and me pulling it just to get it up and over some stretches. It wasn't smooth or easy, but we were moving and progressing.

The highlight of the day was reaching Crazy Well Pool. We took it in turns to strip down to our underwear and go swimming while the other sat with Rivi on the shore.

About 3km (1.9 miles) from the car, we reached a crossroads where we'd intended to camp. It was only early afternoon, though, because we'd started our day so early and walked considerably quicker as Rivi was happier and needed fewer stops. There was no shade and it was a hot

↥ The proud faces of parents who managed to get their baby to sleep and now get to eat their dinner in peace!

afternoon, so we decided to push on to the car and headed home that evening. We spent the whole drive back talking about future adventures and what we wanted to do next. That night, we all enjoyed one of my favourite parts of an adventure: going home. The hot bath, a delicious dinner, resting your tired legs on the sofa and that first night back in your own bed ... was it always this comfy?!

Before going to bed, I quickly updated my social media pages. I wrote: 'This was my first adventure in *such* a long time. It re-ignited something I hadn't realised I was missing. Maybe spontaneity. Or taking on a challenge. Or just properly being out in the wild. I felt free and relaxed and myself again ... all new parents need an adventure!!'

HIKING WITH INFANTS
AND TODDLERS

It can be pretty intimidating heading out for a walk with a small child, especially when going solo. The biggest difference in hiking with an infant or toddler versus an older child is that you will have to carry them for some (assuming your toddler is happy doing a mix of hiking/carrying), if not all, of the hike. As you'll be carrying considerable extra weight, this will limit the distances you'll be able to cover, so be realistic and don't tackle anything too ambitious too soon.

Getting a carrier you find comfortable is vital (or, in our case, we ended up with multiple types of carriers that allowed us the flexibility to get out in different terrains). As with any activity, start small and easy and focus on little and often to adjust your child to being in the carrier and outdoors.

≫→ Everything in nature can be turned into a toy

⤷ Hiking with our Trail Magik carrier. This small and lightweight sling clips onto any bag, giving you great versatility when hiking with toddlers

Then when they are old enough to start wanting to walk stretches on their own, encourage this, even if it makes trekking annoying and slow. In time, you'll be able to build on this and get them accustomed to independent hiking.

Before heading out for a hike, I always double-check my bag to ensure I've got everything I need. My most disastrous hikes have always been when I've forgotten something – when the rain starts and I forgot a water-proof, or there are food demands and I've forgotten a snack, or the tears start and I don't have a dummy.

I've always felt most confident hiking when I have in my pocket several back-ups I can rely on should things kick off. I try to give my daughter a bit of space to settle back down if she starts crying or complaining. If that's not working, and I find my stress levels rising, my priority is finding something to soothe her so I can focus on finishing the walk. My go-to comforters are usually: a snack bar, the dummy, a clip-on toy, singing or telling a story, and, if all else fails, I play her some favourite songs on my phone. On longer hikes, I sometimes even bring toddler headphones so she can listen to her favourite music or a story. Although I prefer her to be getting used to the quiet and being outdoors, sometimes it's more important that I have a relaxing and quiet walk and can make the experience as positive as possible.

If you have greater distances to cover, or you just want a peaceful hike for your well-being, walking while they nap can be a brilliant win-win solution. Most children sleep really well in a sling or buggy on the move, and you can stretch your legs and cover some miles without the constant stops.

THINKING CREATIVELY

Doing longer distances on trails with babies and infants often requires you to think creatively or outside the box – as we did when we used the off-road buggy and a bike trail. We hadn't heard of any other families doing this and didn't know the trail, so were just using our initiative.

There are usually solutions that can make an adventure happen. This could be doing two trips back and forth from your camp spot if it's not too far from the car and the gear is too much to carry in one go. Or getting another adult to join the trip to help carry the load. Or caching items ahead of time so you don't have to carry them all with you. (We wish we'd done this with our Dartmoor adventure – we could have driven to a spot on the trail ahead of our adventure and hidden water somewhere to save us having to carry it all from the start. This could also be done with food supplies or nappies.)

CARRIER OPTIONS

You will likely want to have some form of a carrier for hiking until your children are around four or five when they can start to cover bigger distances by themselves (an experienced four- to five-year-old hiker can usually cover anywhere between 3.4–8km (2–5 miles).

There are three different types of carriers:

OFF-ROAD BUGGY

These buggies have three wheels with large, thick tyres and sometimes also suspension, making them suitable for bumpy off-road terrain. We use an Out'n'About buggy, which has been well-used for day hikes, multi-day treks, festivals and trail running. It's durable, comfortable to use and glides over tough terrain surprisingly easily.

You'll still be somewhat limited with an off-road buggy as it can't go

≫→ Our Out'n'About off-road buggy loaded up for a four-day hiking and wild camping adventure

Essential kit when hiking with an infant or toddler

- extra warm clothes and a warm hat
- sun cream and sun hat
- waterproofs
- snacks and water
- first aid kit and any medication
- fully charged phone in a waterproof bag
- emergency comforters! (dummy, clip-on toy, music, etc)
- (if needed) nappies, eco-baby wipes, eco-nappy bags

*Remember: always tell someone the hike you plan to do and what time you expect to be home.

⚘ Hiking with a Magik carrier

through many kissing gates (unless you're prepared to take the baby out, fold up the buggy to get it through the gate and then reload the baby – not ideal if the buggy is full of camping gear) or over stiles (unless you are happy to lift it over, although this will require extra adults to help). It also can't handle steep or very rocky terrain. However, their huge advantage is that they carry the weight for you (rather than you having to carry the child on your back), allowing you to go for longer hikes or carry more gear, such as camping items. Bungee cords are your go-to for attaching items to a buggy.

When planning off-road buggy routes, look for green (easy) mountain bike trails. An example is the South Downs Way, a 161km (100-mile) trail in the South of England. This trail is suitable for hikers and cyclists, meaning there are no stiles, and the terrain is manageable for off-road tyres.

CHILD CARRIER BACKPACK

There are several child carrier backpacks on the market. These large rucksacks combine a sit-on carrier for your baby/toddler and storage space.

We use an Osprey Poco LT, which comes with some great benefits, such as an in-built sun shade and a frame that means the bag (with your child in) will stay upright if you place it on the ground. It can carry children from six months until they reach age four or 18kg (40lb).

Child carrier backpacks give you great flexibility for walking on all terrain. As the child sits on your back, the carrying adult has complete

visibility and mobility. They come with some negatives, however. All the weight of the child and your gear is concentrated on your back, they are very bulky, and if your toddler decides to get out and walk for a bit, you're left carrying an empty child carrier, which can feel awkward with the weight of any gear you're carrying oddly distributed. They also have very limited storage space. This is fine for a day hike, but for camping or longer hikes, you'll need to rely on other adults to help you carry more gear.

←« The Osprey Poco carries a baby or toddler but also has a large compartment for carrying extra items

SLING CARRIER

Without a doubt, the most helpful bit of hiking kit we own is our Trail Magik sling carrier. This clever attachment packs down small, is lightweight and can be used for children aged from one year to 9.5kg (21lb). When you want to carry your child, you clip the sling to the bottom and top handles of your rucksack (it can be any rucksack as long as it has hip straps). Your child then sits in the sling on your front.

The Trail Magik is ideal for hiking with toddlers who will likely do a mix of hiking themselves and needing to be carried. Because it works on any rucksack, it's versatile for your hiking needs, whether you're carrying a small day pack or a large overnight bag.

I've always found the weight distributed between my front and back easier to manage if I'm carrying a heavy bag and a toddler, and having the child on the front is handy for communicating or feeding them snacks.

Using a sling carrier on a child carrier backpack is possible, meaning you could even carry a baby/toddler on your back and on your front (assuming you are strong enough to manage this sort of weight)! This could be a great option if you have twins or children close in age.

The only negative of a sling carrier is that it can feel a bit awkward carrying a toddler in the front and can obscure your view, making challenging terrain, such as scrambling, more difficult.

JOINING A HIKING COMMUNITY

by Che Ramsden

WE HAVE A JOKE in our family that our son, Joseph, doesn't know that we're not outdoorsy people. Charlotte and I were together for nine years before he was born, and our idea of a good weekend was a decent book or box set. We weren't lazy – we did plenty – we just did it *indoors*. You know, where it's warm, and nothing unexpected happens.

Then, five years ago, Joseph was born. Charlotte remembers her mum saying that your child should spend time outdoors every day because it helps them sleep. But we lived in a second-storey flat; we couldn't simply spend 20 minutes having a cup of tea in the garden, because we didn't have one. To spend any time outdoors, we had to use our legs. That's how it all started.

DISCOVERING MUD IS FUN

When Joseph was six weeks old, Charlotte was back at work and I was given the all-clear after my C-section, so I went for a walk with another new mum. Wellies on and babies strapped to our fronts, we scrambled up the North Downs and frequently stopped, huffing and puffing all the way. I wasn't embarrassed

by my lack of fitness – I'd just had a baby, for goodness' sake, and my new mum friend didn't know I was this unfit before. I was red-faced with the effort and also exhilarated. It was fun to trudge through the mud. I never knew!

'Did you know,' I asked Charlotte later that day, 'that going up the Downs in the mud could be fun?' She looked at me like I was a stranger but, ever supportive, committed to giving it a try.

A few weeks later, I started going for regular walks with my friend, Blaze Trails founder Katy. She'd seen a photo of my six-week postpartum

walk online and assumed I was a 'fellow outdoors mum'. (We were former colleagues; outside of work, we enjoyed dinners and drinks together; she wasn't to know.)

It was a brilliant way to catch up while we were on maternity leave: unlike a parent-and-baby class, going for a walk was about us. Our babies were, for the most part, happily physically connected to us and required minimal attention. So much easier than sitting in a cafe with a fussy baby.

It was a revelation to me that being outdoors was as good for me as it was for the baby. Going for a walk and chatting with other parents always made me feel and sleep better. I was hooked pretty quickly. Charlotte was, too.

WALKING: A LIFELINE

I spent the rest of my maternity leave walking with other new parents once a week. At the weekend, we would do at least one long walk as a family, when Charlotte and I could share the baby carrying and explore the countryside. We committed to doing this no matter the weather. About a year later, we found ourselves up Leith Hill in an icy cold wind, Joseph looking like a Teletubby in several layers and an all-in-one snowsuit, all of us grinning like idiots.

It did wonders for my mental health, and I learned about my body both by talking to other women, by using it and by enjoying using it in this way. It had the added, not-to-be-underestimated benefit that Joseph loved the outdoors and slept much better when we'd been out. (Lest we sound smug, he was a terrible sleeper and, now aged five, still does not sleep through the night.)

Walking was a lifeline. Being in nature and together helped us to hold on to who we are and what we have. Being part of a growing network of parent-and-baby walkers during this time through Blaze Trails meant we had a community to tap into when we wanted to. Conversations quickly ran deep while we walked side-by-side and shared our experiences.

I realised how much our lives had changed when we started planning our holidays. We choose where to go based on the landscape and walks we'd like to try. Isle of Skye in the rain? Lovely! We won't get too hot going up the hills with a large backpack. Lake District in February? Pack a couple of extra layers. Our wardrobes are now half-full of waterproofs.

ADAPTING AS THEY GROW OLDER

We had to reluctantly adjust our expectations of what a family walk is when it became silly to keep a very large and very much no-longer-a-toddler Joseph in the back carrier. 'A walk' no longer means many miles in a few hours with sandwiches along the way and a pub at the end; it's now carrying many sticks for many hours while walking pretty much down the road. What would have been a morning out has become a whole-day activity.

Walking with, rather than carrying, Joseph, has meant a role reversal in lots of ways. He gets hot and needs fewer layers. Meanwhile, we feel we are moving at a snail's pace and tuck mini hot water bottles in our gloves. He encourages us when we get stiff and cheers us along.

But letting Joseph lead outdoors has had unexpected benefits: a slower pace means we notice a lot more of what's around us and how much the same small spots change depending on the hour or the season. Everything is more imaginative and adventurous – suddenly, there are dragons' beds to be made, rocks to be trapped by, 'escape routes' to try, and new songs to be sung.

JOINING AN OUTDOOR COMMUNITY

Getting up in the morning, getting yourself and your child dressed, and making it out the door should be considered major achievements when you're a parent. I don't want to minimise how hard it can be to get out, let alone to get some exercise. Adding something new to the mix can be incredibly daunting – especially if you're not an outdoorsy person.

The great thing about finding a community that also exists online is that you can 'meet' people virtually and ask questions – or at least have a look through the questions others have asked. You can get a sense of what the walk organiser is like and share what might concern you about joining a walk.

I have a notoriously bad sense of direction (in hindsight, probably due to my lack of interest in the outdoors for most of my life), so joining a walking group was ideal. Someone else had planned and would lead the route, while I knew that I'd get to spend the time chatting to an interesting person. I really missed adult conversation – I even missed work! – so this was probably the most important part for me.

The first time you meet another parent or group of parents for a walk can be pretty nerve-wracking. A rough night or a difficult few days can make a seasoned parent walker feel like it's their first time again. But having a walk in the diary and committing to it by clicking 'attend' or telling someone to expect you is a great motivator.

I can safely say that no matter how nervous I was before heading out for a walk, the welcome I received and camaraderie I experienced from other parents once I was there put me at ease pretty quickly. I was once running 15 minutes late after a poonami, so I dropped the others a message. Turns out another person was even later, and those at the starting point on time would get some extra snacks, feed their children, have a natter and an extra trip to the

loo while they waited. While we all aimed to be on time, babies' tummies and bottoms are unpredictable, and the least we could offer each other was some understanding.

I am absolutely the kind of person who doesn't take enough (any) snacks, but guess what? When you're walking with other people it doesn't matter! They will share! And one of them won't have brought enough nappies or will rely on your patience and a balancing hand as they attempt an outdoor change for the first time. You get to help each other, smile at each other and, best of all, suspend all judgement. It's what I imagine a team sport is like, but without any prerequisite skills.

I met all sorts of people through Blaze Trails who had made very different decisions about those early months of parenting, from birth choices to feeding to sleep routines to relationships. We had different outlooks on work and life, but we shared a connection as we trundled on through the mud – both physical and metaphorical.

TACKLING MOUNTAINS

Climbing a mountain can give you the most satisfied of feelings – wild spaces, tangible challenge and the best views. It's a pretty daunting activity to do with children, though. Mountains are big, exposed, have unpredictable weather and don't always have easy get-outs. For this reason, when hiking mountains, you should always hike well within the remit of your fitness and experience.

For our first family mountain climb, we picked the easiest route in the area we were staying in: Sugar Loaf (596m/1,955ft) in Bannau Brycheiniog/the Brecon Beacons, Wales. We did the hike with Dulcie (aged seven), Cooper (aged five) and Rivi (aged two). For all of them, it was their first-ever mountain walk.

The route was simple. We parked in a National Park car park and followed the track straight up and down to the summit, using a mapping app on our phone to navigate. The route covered 2.6km (1.6 miles) and 240m (787ft) of ascent.

We'd been getting the kids hyped about the walk for about a day, showing them the route we'd be taking and talking about what it might be like. Without a doubt, the most important factor for the older two was the promise of snacks! We'd taken them to a supermarket first thing in the morning where they'd been allowed to choose any sweets they wanted ('OK ... well, maybe not the giant-sized marshmallows Cooper as they need to fit in my pocket!'). We'd promised them that on the walk, they could pick a marker – a boulder, a bush, etc – and they could both eat a sweet when they reached it. This tactic worked really well, and everyone bounded up to the summit (Rivi being carried in a child carrier rucksack).

Most of the hike was in conditions with poor visibility and, as we reached the top, the wind picked up and the temperature dropped considerably. Finding a sheltered spot, we wrapped everyone up in all the layers we'd brought, got them all to hydrate and ate some more substantial food.

The way back down was much more challenging than the up, especially for Cooper, whose energy levels suddenly dropped about 500m (0.3 miles) from our car. I quickly whipped out a game – the A–Z Challenge (see page 314) – and was amazed at how effectively it distracted the kids from their tired legs.

Our first mountain climb had gone well. Gil and I both agreed that the hardest part had been taking turns carrying Rivi in the backpack. We wished we'd brought a sling instead (in the sling, her weight sits closer to your body, making it more comfortable to carry her over longer distances) and hiking poles to help take the weight off our knees.

All three kids were asleep in the back of the car within 20 minutes of leaving the car park. Who knew car journeys with three kids could be so peaceful?!

Reaching the summit of
Sugar Loaf, Brecon Beacons

TEN EASY FAMILY-FRIENDLY MOUNTAINS

1 SNOWDON, SNOWDONIA (1,085M/3,560FT)

The highest mountain in Wales has easy-to-follow tracks up and down, as well as a handy coffee shop on the summit and even a train to take you down if you don't want to hike (check opening times).

2 SLEMISH, COUNTY ANTRIM (437M/1,434FT)

Rising abruptly from its flat surrounds, Slemish is an unmissable landmark in Northern Ireland. A short, steep climb with spectacular views.

3 PEN Y GHENT, YORKSHIRE (694M/2,277FT)

The shortest of Yorkshire's popular three peaks, this is a moderate 9.7km (6-mile) loop. The hike is mostly a gentle climb although some scrambling over rocks is required towards the top of the climb.

4 YES TOR, DEVON (619M/2,031FT)

One of the highest mountains in Dartmoor. Start and end the hike at Meldon Reservoir.

5 BEN A'AN, TROSSACHS (461M/1,512FT)

This beautiful hike in Scotland is a 7.2km (4.5-mile) round trip from the car park up a steep and strenuous path.

6 MAM TOR, DERBYSHIRE (517M/1,696FT)

This walk offers some of the Peak District's finest views. From the car park, do an easy there-and-back 3.2km (2-mile) walk or a slightly longer 4.8km (3-mile) circular walk.

7 CAT BELLS, CUMBRIA (451M/1,480FT)

This is a modest summit in the Lake District but will still give you a great sense of achievement and some spectacular views. It's steep in places but easy to climb.

8 PEN Y FAN, MONMOUTHSHIRE (886M/2,907FT)

The most popular mountain in Bannau Brycheiniog/the Brecon Beacons. A strenuous 6.4km (4-mile) hike on well-made footpaths.

9 CONIC HILL, LOCH LOMOND (361M/1,184FT)

A bite-sized walk up a hill overlooking Loch Lomond, Scotland, with great views.

10 CADER IDRIS, SNOWDONIA (893M/2,930FT)

A straightforward but strenuous 9.7km (6-mile) hike from Dôl Idris Car Park. This hike includes trekking through woodland and a rocky scramble.

HIKING BEN NEVIS

by Craig Moffat
. . . .

www.themoffatfamilyadventures.com | @TheMoffatFamilyAdventures

I WORK FULL-TIME, so quality time with the kids is very important to me. I live on the East Coast of Scotland in a little town called Prestonpans with my partner Joanna – the backbone of our family – and our two amazing kids, Faye (aged three) and Cameron (aged nine months).

Family life is very busy, and days can roll into one. We try never to lose sight of our priorities now in life: our kids. It's super important that we give our kids quality time so we can have fun together, learn together and bond together as a family. Getting out and having adventures in the outdoors, whether they are big multi-day trips or just playing in the park, gives us that freedom to explore our relationships in a very real, relaxed environment (unless, of course, we're at the top of a mountain and the wind is blowing a hoolie with horizontal rain!).

We've had many adventures as a family, but I've also enjoyed taking Faye alone (Cameron needs to be a few months older before he can join us). It became apparent very early after Faye joined our family that she loves the outdoors, and I found myself bonding with her over this shared passion in a way I never dreamed possible.

SHARING MY LOVE OF ADVENTURE WITH FAYE

At around 12 months old, Faye summited her first Munro in the Cairngorms area (Munros are Scottish mountains above 914m/3,000ft). By age three, she had completed 20 Munros, including Ben Nevis. We'd also hiked up Pico Viejo in Tenerife, which has a height of 3,135m (10,285ft), and conquered Scafell Pike, England's highest mountain at 978m (3,209ft).

Together, we've explored and climbed mountains, kayaked, paddleboarded and hiked along beaches. We also love camping together. Our first multi-night camping trip was on the Isle of Mull on an idyllic campsite based on the West Coast, a stone's throw away from Iona. We packed up and headed on a two-hour drive to Oban to catch the big ferry to Mull. We stayed at Fidden Farm, a gem of a campsite. The site has a huge field verging on to a white beach looking out to the clear blue sea. We had such a chilled time together there, and Faye met a couple from Aberdeen in the tent beside us. Meeting lots of friendly people willing to spend time with the kids is one of the things I consistently love about our adventures. Every day, Faye would go over and see our new friends, and every night Faye would go over and say goodnight. It really warmed my heart to see the interaction.

We also got the ferry to Iona one day, visited the abbey and played on the many beaches. I'll always remember Faye stirring a pot of cheesy pasta on the stove, looking out to the sea. Precious memories were made that will stay with me for ever.

PLANNING AND GETTING OUT THE DOOR

Getting out on our adventures together always starts way before we even plan what we want to do. Scotland is a beautiful country, but to truly explore the lesser-trodden path, the kids need to be comfortable with longer drives. This is important. We took the kids out in the car from a young age and built up the distance travelled. I had a map I would open when planning, and I knew how far we could go based on Faye's tolerance for travelling in the car. When Faye was one, we could drive anywhere within a two-hour stretch; anything over, and Faye would get car sick. At three, Faye can now travel more than six hours with stops. If it's longer then we book a hotel and split the journey.

When purchasing kit, I find it essential to do a lot of research as this kit will support the family in having great, enjoyable days out. For instance, I spent two weeks researching what child carrier to get and tried a few in a shop. It needed to be sturdy and fill me with confidence when hiking, have enough storage room for big days out, and more than anything, Faye and Cameron needed to feel comfortable in it. In the end, I settled on an Osprey Poco Plus pack with the essential rain cover.

My advice with any kit is to borrow from a friend if possible so you can try it before you buy. When we were teaching Faye how to paddleboard, I purchased three different life vests before I was happy with the safest, most important piece of kit for the water. We went for the Vine Kids Swim Vest/float jacket.

Planning is key to making our adventures a success. It's important to keep your main goal in mind – for me, this is ensuring Faye and Cameron enjoy whatever adventure we are on. It should be safe, and if there is any risk, this is reduced to a manageable level. The one prerequisite to any adventure is if Faye or Cameron (when he is bigger) says they want to stop, then we stop. No questions asked and no pressure to continue.

This does and will happen. I remember once we were climbing a Munro called Meall a' Choire Lèith in the Cairngorms in winter conditions and were only around 20 minutes from the end of a two-hour hike when Faye got upset, asking for her mummy, and was adamant she wanted to go back to the car. I turned with no regret and we made our way down. I need to ensure Faye is not pushed into a situation she doesn't want to be in; this is how we build trust within our relationships.

On our mountain adventures – where the risk is often greater – I plan nap times and snack stops, and if the weather deteriorates, I have a plan B. I always ensure someone knows our route and estimated times, use the safest route possible and stick to turnaround times. I also always have all the necessary safety equipment. From a safety perspective, when hiking, we know how to use a map and compass and run two GPS devices at the same time, one to back the other up. I always carry survival shelters, foil blankets, a first aid kit, spare clothes (taking extra in case the kids have an accident) and LED flares. This list is not exhaustive, and there is plenty of advice online, so do your research.

As with any plan, things won't always go right, and we must know that's OK and make it part of the adventure. Some of our biggest learnings in parenthood come when we face challenges and learn how to overcome them. Personally, I'd say the biggest challenge is getting to understand your kids and when they are up for an adventure or just want to enjoy playing in the back garden. Most other challenges I find are behavioural. For example, Faye decided halfway up Ben Nevis that she wanted to slide down a banking of snow; unknown to her, the banking had a steep cliff edge. She couldn't understand why daddy wouldn't let her. When I said no, and she got upset, instead of getting her back in the pack, I sat with her and tried to explain as best I could the reasons why she couldn't slide down it. Five minutes later, we were happily on our way.

OUR BIGGEST ADVENTURE

Faye and I had been building our mountain days up for our biggest challenge: climbing Ben Nevis in aid of Glasgow Children's Hospital Charity. Our goal was to raise funds and awareness of the great work the charity and hospital do. We also have family who are alive today because of them; this hike was for Owen and Lucy.

Ben Nevis is 1,345m (4,411ft) tall and is a long climb that's especially notorious for difficult weather. There were several challenges to overcome,

including Faye spending prolonged periods of time in the pack and setting a target for her to walk at least 10 per cent of the route. We also needed to have extra safety and spare kit to do this hike safely with a toddler, which added substantial weight to the pack.

We stayed a couple of days beforehand in a little bothy to get used to our surroundings and allow Faye to settle and enjoy the area after the four-hour journey to get there. It was a beautiful sunny morning in July when we left the Ben Nevis Visitor Centre car park with the challenge in full view in front of us. I had broken the hike into three sections. The first, from the car park to the lochan (freshwater lake). The second, from the lochan to the summit plateau. And finally, the summit itself.

By mid-morning, we had reached the start of the second section, and Faye had done her little Highland dance via Facebook Live to celebrate! We had reached the summit plateau by 11.30am and at this point, I was feeling it in the legs. I remember I grunted a little with the effort, and Faye quickly let me know, 'it's going to be OK; we're nearly there.'

My own daughter, at just two years old, motivating me!

We reached the summit by noon, and we were buzzing. Faye knew she had accomplished something amazing. We spent half an hour at the top, speaking to people and collecting donations. We sat at the peak in sunny, warm conditions. Faye was lapping up the attention from fellow hikers wanting to know what we were doing. I was sitting with an overwhelming feeling of pride and happiness on top of Ben Nevis with my daughter – a feeling I still get emotional thinking about today.

The hike down was tough, especially on the loose scree. Once we completed it, we treated ourselves to ice cream. We raised over £1,500 and completed the hike in 7 hours and 11 minutes.

INCLUDE OUR CHILDREN IN OUR PASSIONS

It's important to highlight that we, as parents, consciously decided on hobbies that we enjoyed and that made us happy before having kids. Starting a family doesn't mean our hobbies should stop; we should include our children in our passions and watch them flourish, sharing our love for life and adventure. My love for the outdoors now has a greater meaning than ever before; I get far more enjoyment by sharing it with my children.

The very close bond I have with Faye, I believe, comes from our days together building memories outdoors. Although Cameron is now getting to the age where he too can join us on slightly more adventurous activities, don't underestimate the importance of the little adventures in the back garden too – they also count! Our love and attention mould our kids, and the outdoors helps support a positive upbringing. It's why as a family we will always continue to prioritise our adventures!

HIKING BEN NEVIS

MULTI-DAY HIKING

Once you've built your confidence hiking with children, you might be ready to take the step to do multi-day hikes. When planning a family hiking adventure, your success will likely entirely fall on having back-up plans for shortening your distances should your days not work out. This could be having alternate accommodation options or carrying bus timetables so you can shorten distances and use public transport to get you to the next stage if needed.

The first thing I do whenever I plan a multi-day hike is order some guidebooks from my local library – in them, you'll find maps, lists of accommodation and top tips for easy planning.

The thing that will determine how you plan and pack is the accommodation you choose. There are two options: 'bed' accommodation such as hostels, hotels and huts; or camping. You may wish to use a combination.

HOTELS, HOSTELS AND HUTS

You can complete many trails without needing to camp, staying in a mixture of hotels, hostels and Airbnbs each night. This can take a lot of planning as you'll probably need to book these in advance – especially if you are hiking on a popular trail or in peak season. You'll also need to accept that this will often come with additional distance, as rarely will you find all the accommodation you need directly on the trail. Buses or taxis might help you shorten these additional miles, but again, this option will take extra planning (and will cost more money).

Another option is to set up a base for your hike and yo-yo back and forth to your accommodation each morning and night. If there's a good network in the area, you might

»→ ⚘ Glamping in a safari tent at Nature's Nest, Wye Valley

←« Off-grid camping in the woods

be able to rely on a mixture of trains and buses. Most likely, though, you'll need to pre-book taxis or rely on a two-car system (you both drive to the end of the day's hike to leave one car there before driving in the other car to the start – you reverse the process at the end of the day). This can be time-consuming and obviously requires two vehicles.

While not so common in the UK, many trails offer hut-to-hut hiking in Europe. Huts are regularly spaced along the trail offering an affordable place to stay and, usually, a simple warm meal at the end of the day. The huts offer shared bunk-rooms (which might not be ideal if you have an infant) and require you to bring a sleeping bag. There is also huge networks of trails, such as the Camino de Santiago, which offer guest room accommodation in the form of *albergues*. These lodging houses are dotted around the villages you pass through, and when you've finished hiking, you pick an *albergue* and pay a reasonable price for board and food.

The biggest advantage to using hotels and hostels is that you can keep your carrying weight to a minimum as you don't need to bring tents and other camping items. They also give you a comfy bed and a warm shower each night, which can help with morale and recovery, especially on bad-weather days.

This option will be expensive, though, as trail accommodation options are usually limited and, therefore, pricier. You also don't have much

⚡ Staying in a glamping pod at Secret Valley glamping site near Bridgwater

Every car journey is an opportunity to stop mid-way and find a little piece of nature to explore on a short walk

flexibility as you'll need to make bookings in advance. With this in mind, it's best to plan a route with short, manageable daily distances and maybe also a rest day factored into the middle to give you the option to make up miles if you fall behind.

If you are struggling with the logistics of booking accommodation, several providers offer self-guided walking holidays. They will book all the accommodation and provide maps and you hike alone at your own pace. Just do an internet search to find one that suits your needs.

CAMPING

Combining hiking and camping can feel like a huge adventure and a great way to get close to nature. You could use designated campsites, wild camps or a combination.

The biggest challenge with multi-day camping adventures with children is carrying all the gear. As well as all your clothes, first aid kit, food and water, you've also got a tent, sleeping mats and sleeping bags to consider. In addition, you have all the extra items your children might need (such as nappies or comforters), and maybe even a child to carry if you're going with an infant or toddler.

For shorter multi-day camping hikes, we've managed to carry a toddler and all the gear needed using rucksacks and a sling or child carrier backpack. We've found using an off-road buggy to be the easiest option for longer treks, as you can pile it high with all your gear. This greatly limits the routes you can take, though, as they need to be suitable for wheels.

One of the biggest advantages of camping is that it gives you complete flexibility. Most campsites don't need to be booked in advance (double-check this for your trail as some do during busy periods), meaning you can adapt your plan as you hike.

If you're wild camping, it can get tough after a few days with no showers, so generally, we always break up wild camping after three days with a campsite to refresh and ditch our rubbish (especially important if you're carrying dirty nappies – they can get smelly and heavy!).

COMBO ACCOMMODATION

Combining camping and bed accommodation might give you the best of both worlds, allowing you to camp out in the wild while also having a comfortable break and a chance to refresh in a room once in a while.

BAGGAGE TRANSFER

Most trails in the UK offer baggage transfer services. You pay a provider (often a taxi company) to pick up your bags each morning and drop them at your next accommodation ahead of your arrival. This saves you carrying all your gear, making hiking with children considerably easier.

You'll need to know exactly where you're staying each night and factor in extra in your budget to pay for the service. To find a baggage transfer on your trail, do an internet search. Providers are also usually listed on the trail's official website.

PACKING AND FITTING RUCKSACKS

If you are carrying your gear, packing and fitting your rucksacks properly will considerably decrease the chances of injury and discomfort for all the family.

Generally, children shouldn't carry more than 20 per cent of their bodyweight; for those under eight, this should be less. If you have children who are walking (rather than being carried) and capable, then getting them to carry some items, even if just their own snacks and waterproofs, can help take the burden off the adults. If they lean forwards when they walk, it is usually a sign that the weight is too much for them.

Rucksacks should all be the correct size for the person carrying them and come with a hip strap to help distribute the bag's weight. All straps should be clipped up, and you need to adjust the bag so the weight mostly sits on the hips and not on the shoulders. When your child adjusts their bag, hold the bottom of the rucksack 5cm (2in) above the waist, keeping the top just below the base of the skull. Bags usually come with fitting instructions or go to any outdoor shop and the assistants will show you how to fit it correctly.

When packing a bag, put heavy items at the bottom, close to the back and evenly distributed. Have snacks and a water bottle that are easy to access in the side or hip pockets. Put a warm layer and waterproofs at the top of the bag so they can be grabbed easily on breaks or if the weather changes suddenly.

FAMILY-FRIENDLY LONG-DISTANCE UK HIKING TRAILS

SOUTH DOWNS WAY, ENGLAND (160KM/100 MILES)

A gentle (but hilly) trail starting in Winchester, Hampshire, and finishing in the seaside resort of Eastbourne, East Sussex. As this is a hiking and cycling trail, it's possible to do the entire route with an off-road buggy. Hotels and campsites are dotted about, although many people have managed the entire trail wild camping. Although not legal, it is generally tolerated if you wild camp by the path.

PEMBROKESHIRE COAST PATH, WALES (300KM/186 MILES)

With *lots* of cliff climbs, this trail is suitable for families wanting more of a challenge. The trail takes you along the stunning Pembrokeshire coastline. Affordable accommodation is limited so you'll need to do some planning in advance. Wild camping is not legal, although is usually tolerated on the trail.

CATERAN TRAIL, SCOTLAND (103KM/64 MILES)

This loop is one of Scotland's Great Trails. The trail has no official start or end and can be joined at any point. It has five stages, although with children you may want to break this down into shorter sections. There are a few hotels and campsites dotted along the trail, although wild camping will give you most flexibility.

CAUSEWAY COAST WAY, NORTHERN IRELAND
(53KM/33 MILES)

You can look forward to dramatic cliffs, sandy beaches and offshore rocks on this trail, which stretches from Portstewart to Ballycastle. The trail has been split into six short, manageable sections, making it ideal for families. There are lots of campsite, hotel and B&B options en route.

THAMES PATH, ENGLAND
(296KM/184 MILES)

This is an excellent trail for families as it's flat the whole way. It stretches from the source in the Cotswolds to London. The Thames Path is well-served by public transport, making it great for section hiking or yo-yoing from a base. There are not many camping options on the trail, so you'll be limited to using hotels and guesthouses.

THE RIDGEWAY, ENGLAND
(140KM/87 MILES)

Described as Britain's oldest road, the Ridgeway passes through rural southern central England. Hotels are sparse on the route. There's no legal right to wild camp, although the National Trail website states that most landowners on the Ridgeway tend not to object to people camping as long as they tidy up after themselves. You are able to cycle on the trail between Avebury and Goring, so in theory this section should be suitable for off-road buggies.

GREAT GLEN WAY, SCOTLAND
(126KM/78 MILES)

The Great Glen Way is a brilliant family-friendly trail, linking Fort William in the south-west to Inverness. The trail follows the lochs, although there are alternative routes if you want more of a challenge and more climbing. You can legally wild camp, or use a mix of hostels, hotels and Airbnbs. The trail is suitable for off-road buggies.

Teaching our kids they can achieve anything

HIKING THE WEST HIGHLAND WAY

by Leanne Woodall

@outdoor_with_the_woodalls | www.outdoorwiththewoodalls.com

WHEN OUR YOUNGEST, Ariya, was born, we began to notice our eldest children, Reo and Niyah, had become addicted to screens and would complain of boredom if ever their iPad batteries died. We have seen how children's mental health can be affected by social media and gaming and wanted the kids to have a balanced childhood. So, we purchased an off-road buggy and began going on buggy-friendly walks as a family.

Initially on walks, the eldest two would complain that they wanted to be home on the Xbox, but we persevered and noticed a huge difference within six months. They adapted so well to our adventures and exploring the outdoors, their behaviour improved, and they took an interest in nature, history and geography. We began to realise the outdoors really was the best place for learning.

By the age of two, Ariya was showing an impressive aptitude for hiking; she had already climbed her first wainwright. It took three times longer than normal as she wanted to pick up every stick and stone we passed, but she walked entirely by herself. This was the start of our true family adventures. The outdoors became an essential part of our weeks – we all became addicted and started going on walking holidays in Scotland, Wales and the Lake District.

Ariya continued to amaze us with her ability to cover long distances without complaint. Before she had turned three, she even climbed Snowdon without needing to be carried!

PREPARING FOR THE WEST HIGHLAND WAY

We came across the West Highland Way (WHW) after visiting Scotland for a road-trip holiday. After researching, I mentioned it to my husband, Reo

The Woodall family's top tips for long-distance family hikes

- Give yourself lots of time for training. Doing this beforehand ensured we could all walk for multiple days, in the rain, wind and cold, and on a variety of terrains.
- Include them in the planning.
- Be flexible and plan your walk around your slowest members.
- Play games such as Eye Spy and The Floor Is Lava.
- Give them each a snack bag that they make up for each day.
- If there are beaches and lakes, take towels and paddle shoes so you can stop and relax.
- Put petroleum jelly on everyone's feet and change socks halfway through the walk to prevent blisters.
- Fit the children in good walking boots they wear for training to minimise sore feet.
- Always walk at kids' pace and don't ever rush them.
- If you're hiking in Scotland: hair nets and midge cream are vital and certainly needed if you walk between May and October!

and Niyah. We all agreed it would be a great challenge and a way to spend quality time together, making memories while raising money for charity. So, I ordered the books, and the planning began.

I knew how important it was to train, so six months before our big adventure, we started walking a few times a week, covering around 16km (10 miles) each day. Then, three months before starting, we hiked every single day, totalling over about 100km (60 miles) a week (our children are home-educated, so we used this training and organising as part of their education).

The training was a great way to see how the kids coped, carrying their own bags and hiking in all weathers. They were only aged ten, eight and three, so we had no expectations at this point, but we gave them the best training and included the older two in all the planning. This helped keep them excited and engaged with what we were doing.

We possibly overpacked, ensuring we were prepared for all scenarios; we had all medications in case of illnesses. In addition to this were extra clothing for warm and colder weather, pre-packed dehydrated meals in case we couldn't get to restaurants or cafes, and a second pair of shoes for everyone to reduce the chances of blisters. These trainers came in useful after heavy rain when we couldn't get our walking boots dry, so the kids wore trainers for a couple of days on the lighter sections of the trail.

We decided to use baggage handlers as our tent and extra supplies were too heavy to carry. This was a great decision and made the trip much easier. The company we used was amazing because, after careful consideration, we

planned to have no plan! Yes, crazy, I know. I knew the route and our ideal daily mileage, but we simply didn't know how much Ariya would be able to cope with each day. Our priority was to make the experience enjoyable. So, the deal was we would never force her to walk, and if she couldn't do it, we would stop. It was therefore essential that we had complete flexibility.

We agreed to let the company know the night before where we would be camping the next day. This also meant taking a chance with accommodation and hoping there was space, but we were always lucky to find somewhere. There were also two occasions when it was chucking it down with rain; everyone was drenched and couldn't face putting up a tent in a wet field. For those nights, we booked into cabins, which made a huge difference in keeping the kids happy and getting the kit dry for the next day.

KEEPING IT MANAGEABLE WITH CHILDREN

The hardest part for us was camping, as more midges would arrive at sunset when we were putting the tent up and at sunrise when we were taking it down. It was also harder to dry clothes in a tent if they got wet. Rain would make the hiking more challenging as we couldn't stop as often as there was little shelter. Ariya just loved to stop all the time when hiking so it was lucky that we only had two days of rain. She managed really well, considering the wet-day walks were 14.5km (9 miles) and 24km (15 miles). Good waterproofs are a must!

Each day, we would wake and say to the kids, 'Right, let's go on another adventure and see if we can spot any animals and find our campsite.' We kept them excited and engaged. They thoroughly enjoyed the sense of adventure.

We gave ourselves two weeks to complete the walk, but we managed it in ten days. Our total mileage, including walking to the campsites, shops and sightseeing, was 209km (130 miles). I still can't believe the kids managed it without complaints, zero blisters or moaning!!

Having ten whole days surrounded by nature, watching our kids fully embrace the outdoors was something we will never forget; we chatted, played games, told stories and sang songs. We had so many people stop and chat with the children, telling them how brilliantly they were doing. We met people from across the world. Reo spent many hours walking with other hikers talking to them about their own countries and the walk itself. Having him turn around and say he hadn't missed the Xbox was the biggest surprise; even now, years later, they regularly wake up and ask if we can go for another hike.

ROCK CLIMBING

WITH CHILDREN

Rock climbing is a fun activity to do with children and a great way for them to learn safety and confidence in the outdoors. Most people first experience climbing in an indoor climbing wall – an easy, cheap and safe way to get to grips with the sport. There are more than 500 climbing centres in the UK, most offering instruction, equipment hire and a friendly atmosphere.

The most logical place to start is on a bouldering wall. As you don't climb very high (and are protected from falling by big, soft crash mats below), you don't need any ropes.

Many indoor climbing and bouldering centres have designated areas just for children, allowing them to start climbing as young as two. Visiting a centre is a brilliant family activity as you can all have a go and take turns trying out different routes (known as 'problems'). For your first session,

←« ⛏ You can start children rock climbing as young as four. Boulder rooms are a great place to start introducing them to the sport

⬆ Rock climbing kit can be expensive. See if you can hire what you need from your local rock climbing centre

I'd suggest paying for an instructor, as getting to grips with rock climbing is a lot to do with technique.

Once you've picked up basic climbing skills and some confidence getting yourself up and down a wall, you may want to progress to climbing outdoors. This can range from bouldering on small rocks and boulders to rock climbing off crags and cliffs. There are also other forms of climbing, including scrambling, ice climbing and mountaineering.

More risks are associated with climbing outdoors as conditions can quickly change and there are greater hazards. Unless you have a very experienced climber in your family, it's best to do outdoor climbing supervised by an instructor.

Rock climbing equipment can be expensive, especially for children who will quickly outgrow their shoes, harnesses and helmets. Hiring from rock climbing centres or instructors might be a cheaper option. Check noticeboards at rock climbing centres for preloved equipment being sold cheaply.

Different types of rock climbing

BOULDERING: Practised on small rocks and boulders either indoors or out.

ROCK CLIMBING: Requires two people and involves climbing with ropes. Can be done indoors or out. The person climbing is attached to a rope that is controlled by the other person. There are two types of roped climbing:

1 **Top roping:** The climber is secured by a rope above so if they fall it won't be far.
2 **Leading:** This is where the rope is trailed by the climber and controlled entirely from below. It requires a higher level of skill and judgement.

ICE CLIMBING: Climbing on ice and snow, roped and using specialist crampons and ice axe equipment. It's mostly done outside although there are now some indoor venues offering ice climbing.

SCRAMBLING: Combines hill walking and rock climbing. Basic scrambling can involve climbing over easy-to-manage rocks. Whereas harder scrambling involves more skills and equipment.

MOUNTAINEERING: Involves walking, scrambling and also sometimes rock and ice climbing over very large mountains.

MULTI-PITCH ROCK CLIMBING

by Alistair Ross

HELEN AND I MET at the climbing club at university; the outdoors has always been a big part of our lives. As we married and had kids, it was inevitable that we'd try and maintain camping, running, walking and climbing as integral to our family life. That is perhaps easier said than done, especially when it comes to climbing.

As the girls have grown older, we've grown bolder with what we can do as a family. It's taken time, but we are proud to feel like climbers again!

STRUGGLING TO ADAPT WITH CHILDREN

Right from Emily's first few weeks, we were outdoors. Taking young babies to the crag is relatively straightforward as you can climb with friends or boulder quite merrily while they snooze or gurgle at the clouds. This all changes pretty rapidly once they can roll, crawl and develop a hunger for eating sheep poo. Suddenly, climbing outings feel like an exhausting task of risk management. As soon as you add a second baby to the equation, it feels like it removes the option of outdoor climbing altogether. The period after Sophie was born and while Helen recovered a second time was probably our biggest hiatus from climbing, let alone outdoor climbing.

When we could, we switched to mostly indoor climbing. It feels like a sensible move since squishy crash mats make for a safer environment for toddling and crawling. Emily and Sophie could start to experience climbing for themselves, both watching and doing. Indoor bouldering certainly makes climbing accessible for young families.

We bought the girls chest harnesses from a very young age, determined to make outdoor climbing work. This relied on us being with other friends or family and finding short, easy climbs to do in

warm, dry weather. We recognise that we built a rod for our own backs by sticking mainly to trad climbing, where we'd want to lead a route for the girls to follow. There is a lot of waiting and watching and this wasn't possible without other adults being around to support.

Overall, before Sophie started school, we probably managed only a couple of days a year at best, visiting accessible haunts such as Stanage Edge, Burbage or Birchen Edge in the Peak District.

PERSEVERING

I think if we reflect on these years, we definitely had times when we didn't feel like climbers any more. Trips were so few and far between that our skills and confidence grew rusty. Helen in particular struggled physically and was quite tough on herself mentally.

There were also days when the girls themselves seemed to hate it. They found it too difficult, or scary, or disheartening, or tiring, or cold. We berated ourselves about whether this was the right thing to do. At this point, Helen and I had climbed together as a couple for a decade – climbing apart from each other, and the girls, wouldn't have seemed right.

Perhaps climbing was just too difficult with a young family, and perhaps we should wait? We were outdoors a lot but climbing just felt like a step too far.

This story would be a lot shorter if it had all ended at this point, but I'm glad

to say we persevered. There were a few things we could cite as being the turning point for us as a climbing family. Emily and Sophie just became that little bit older; old enough to fit rock shoes, to be stronger and taller, to enjoy a challenge and celebrate success. There came a point when they asked to climb. We'd been worried that they might not share our love of climbing. Thankfully, we were wrong.

There are some huge advantages to using indoor climbing walls as a training ground. Unlike outdoors, someone has had the wherewithal to design routes in various colours and shapes to keep everyone entertained. Rock shoes can be hired without worrying about spending excess money on those ever-growing feet. You can go there when it's raining, or after school or for children's parties. They also support rest and allow the girls to sit and read if they don't feel like pushing themselves. Both Emily and Sophie had the confidence and excitement to challenge themselves, and they started to feel inspired about how this would translate outdoors.

We wanted to give our girls a thirst for something more adventurous, like the days climbing Helen and I had experienced years before. Over the spring and summer, when Sophie turned six and Emily eight, we decided to start trying some more ambitious outdoor climbing, starting with our first attempt at a muti-pitch route: the Rowan Route.

ROWAN ROUTE

We picked our first multi-pitch route carefully. We ended up at the bottom of Rowan Route on Milestone Buttress in Eryri, North Wales. This is quite close to roadside parking, so it wasn't too far to walk in to the climbing. This was important because we knew this would be an ambitious undertaking for the girls, so we didn't want to add a monster hike to the start and end of the day.

The route also has an easy grade (Diff, if you know climbing grades) but on sound rock that can be readily protected safety-wise with traditional gear. And between pitches, there were big ledges with space for several people to sit comfortably.

The descent was the thing we questioned the most with our choice. So many multi-pitch routes in the mountains contain either a big walk off the top in another direction once you finish the last pitch or you have a scramble or down-climb of an easy route back to the bottom, which would have been difficult to make safe with children. We chose Milestone because it avoided both of these things; but this didn't mean the descent would be easy!

No matter how hard you try to be organised, it's never an early start with kids. By climbing standards, we were at the crag quite late in the day – so late we had lunch before even starting. What that did mean was that we could chat with other people setting off on the route ahead of us, one being a dad and his teenage daughters, who were leading for the first time – a completely new challenge that would be ahead of Emily and Sophie in the future if they choose.

How we climb as a family seems to work well for the girls and us. It will likely change in future, and other families may need to find different combinations that work for them. Both Helen and I can and do lead climb, probably myself more so historically, particularly on harder routes. But right now, we find it works better for Helen to lead and belay from the top while I offer assistance by climbing close to the girls. We opted to use double ropes on Rowan Route, with Emily seconding independently up to Helen before belaying myself and Sophie together on the other rope afterwards.

Emily was always within hearing distance of either me at the bottom or Helen at the top of a pitch. She found the climbing itself fairly straightforward, which is exactly what we wanted when doing something bigger where she needed the confidence to climb independently, and we also needed to move quickly enough to do several pitches in one afternoon. Sophie had fun seconding, and I was able to give her lots of space to be independent, helping

only when we were working out how to take out the protection.

The big downside to climbing multi-pitch routes as a four is the waiting around while Helen was leading and setting up belays. The ledges were comfortable enough, and everyone stayed tied on to keep safe. Basic things are definitely more exciting while halfway up a rock face, especially negotiating a harnessed-up wee stop with young girls! More importantly, there were Rolos, and who doesn't love Rolos?!

Everyone had a real sense of achievement on reaching the top. No one had got upset, the ropes weren't in a tangle, and it was still daylight. But we still had to make our way down. The descent from Milestone Crag is a gully to one side. This can be climbed down by experienced climbers, although it can be quite damp at any time of year. We opted for a roped descent. Helen abseiled first, travelling the full length of our 50m (164ft) rope to get as far down as possible. Sophie was then an absolute superstar for being lowered on belay all the way down to Helen, followed by Emily. There was not a complaint to be heard, but there was also no choice; they trusted us, had the skills, and knew exactly how to get on with it.

A bit of easy scrambling later, we were back at the bags and then it was just a short walk back to the car as the sun set. It was a later finish than we'd imagined, but the girls were chuffed with fish and chips and a giant chocolate cookie at 9pm!

Ideally, we'd have had a long lie-in the following day, but hey, they're kids and were up at the crack of dawn at the campsite and ready to head out for a bike ride...

Our first multi-pitch route was a huge success and has given us the confidence to do more, including climbing Harborough Rocks, Dovestone Tor and off the beaches of the Gower Peninsula. The Gower is an especially great haunt for family climbing in the UK: single-pitch, easy climbing routes straight off the sandy beach. The girls made sandcastles and turned cartwheels in the sunshine between routes.

Of all the climbing we've ever done with our girls, it is the multi-pitch route that has stuck in their memory the most due to its greater sense of adventure. Emily and Sophie are now involved in picking their next adventure route to climb. We're proud of how we've adapted and persevered, sharing our passions with our girls and maintaining our dream of climbing together as a family.

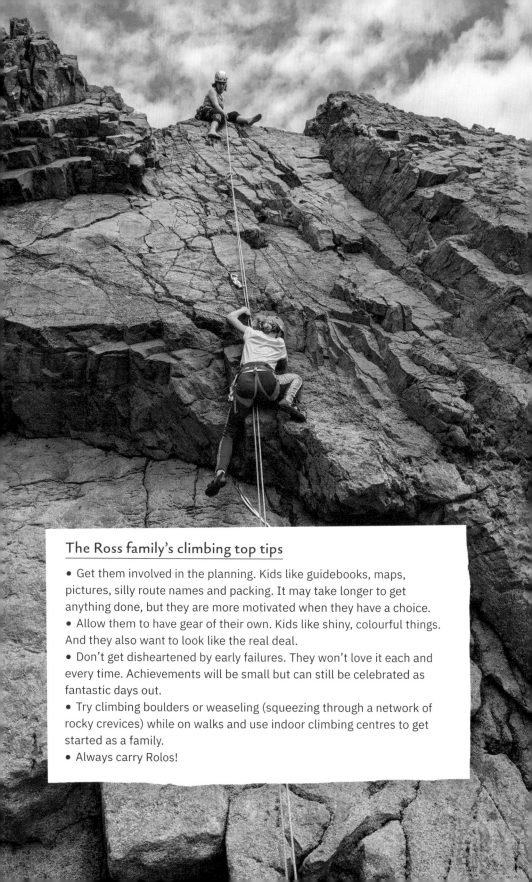

The Ross family's climbing top tips

• Get them involved in the planning. Kids like guidebooks, maps, pictures, silly route names and packing. It may take longer to get anything done, but they are more motivated when they have a choice.
• Allow them to have gear of their own. Kids like shiny, colourful things. And they also want to look like the real deal.
• Don't get disheartened by early failures. They won't love it each and every time. Achievements will be small but can still be celebrated as fantastic days out.
• Try climbing boulders or weaseling (squeezing through a network of rocky crevices) while on walks and use indoor climbing centres to get started as a family.
• Always carry Rolos!

SNOW ADVENTURES

In the heart of winter, it can be hard to find adventures to keep the family busy ... unless you get into snow sports! Although the UK isn't perhaps best-known for its snow sports, Scotland has some well-established resorts, with even a few snow clubs in England. Kids intuitively love snow. With soft falls, snow fights and snow angels on the agenda, there's loads of fun to be had, whether downhill skiing or snowboarding, snowshoeing or cross-country skiing.

Keeping them warm and dry is the key to getting out in the snow with children; as is knowing when to call it a day to all head home for warmth and dry clothes. Good-quality waterproofs and base layers are essential – remember not to overdress them, so they get sweaty once they start getting active. Take plenty of warm layers, dry spare clothes and a hot flask of soup or drink for breaks.

Gloves will be important and will get wet, so it's worth packing a spare to change halfway through the session. Everyone will also need eye protection; low-light goggles are generally more suitable than sunglasses. Also, smother your children (and you) in lots of sunscreen, even on a cloudy day.

If you're starting out in any snow sport, joining a club is a good way to find information, learn about the equipment and make friends.

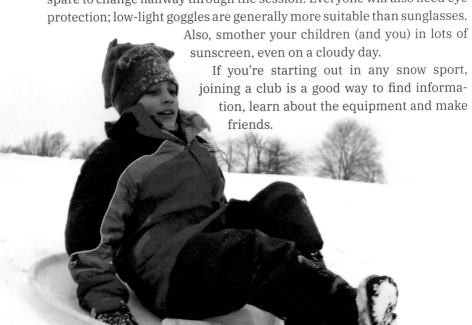

WHERE TO GO SKIING AND SNOWBOARDING

The UK has five Scottish ski resorts and four English club fields:

SCOTLAND

Glenshee Ski & Snowboard, Aberdeenshire, Scotland (www.ski-glenshee .co.uk): Claims to have the most extensive skiing areas in the UK; a total of 40km (25 miles) of downhill mountains covering four mountains.

Lecht 2090, Aberdeenshire, Scotland (www.lecht.co.uk): One of the smaller resorts but a great choice for families with shorter runs ideal for beginners. Lecht stands at 637m (2,090ft) above sea level offering amazing views of the Cairngorms National Park.

Cairngorm Mountain Scotland, Aviemore, Scotland (www.cairngorm mountain.co.uk): A popular resort that's been running for more than 50 years. There are 11 lifts, and a funicular railway to transport you to the mountain top. There's also a reindeer centre just down the road, which is a great activity for the family when you need a rest from snow sports (www.cairngormreindeer.co.uk).

Nevis Range Mountain Experience, Fort William, Scotland (www.
nevisrange.co.uk): This offers plenty of runs available for beginners, as
well as easy access to the backcountry for more experienced skiers and
boarders. There is also a dry slope for when there is insignificant snow
cover, and their lower mountain bike tracks are open all season.

Glencoe Mountain, Argyll, Scotland (www.glencoemountain.co.uk):
Boarders and skiers of all levels are catered for at Glencoe with 20 runs
of varying grades and eight different lifts.

ENGLAND

Ski-Allenheads, Northumberland, England (www.ski-allenheads.co.uk):
A membership-based slope with tows in place that welcomes all abilities
and is a good choice for beginners.

Weardale Ski Club, County Durham, England (www.skiweardale.com):
Relying on volunteers, this basic club includes two permanent button
tows and two storey ski lodge and workshop.

Lake District Ski Club, Cumbria, England (www.ldscsnowski.co.uk): This
has some of the best snow conditions in the Lake District, with a button
lift available and nine pistes, the longest being 1.6km (1 mile) in length.
Not suitable for young families, as it's about an hour's steep hike to
reach Raise, and the skiing is on tough, rugged terrain.

Yad Moss, Cumbria, England (www.yadmoss.co.uk): Yad Moss has
the longest single-button lift in England and is suitable only for
intermediate and advanced skiers and snowboarders.

UK'S BEST INDOOR SNOW CENTRES

The UK also has a great network of indoor dry slopes and snow centres
offering real-snow runs. Indoor snow centres are a great place to try
skiing and snowboarding before hitting the slopes. They are also a good
back-up if the weather conditions aren't right for doing it outdoors.

SNOWSHOEING

Snowshoeing is probably the easiest and cheapest way for a family to enjoy getting out in the snow and usually doesn't require lessons to learn – just safe knowledge of snow conditions and a bit of practice. Wearing snowshoes spreads the wearer's weight, enabling you to travel on top rather than through the snow, keeping your legs dry and making it easier to cover longer distances.

Youth snowshoes are usually one-size-fits-all, measured by weight categories rather than foot size. Once your child is over 36kg (79lb), snowshoes designed for women may become the best-fitting. Snowshoes should ideally be worn with insulated lightweight winter boots and fitted snuggly but not so tight that they'll cause discomfort.

Gaiters are worn on the lower part of your leg to create a seal between the top of your boot and the bottom of your trousers. It's a good idea to fit gaiters on children when snowshoeing as they will inevitably sink a few inches (and will want to mess around in the snow sometimes) and this will help keep them dry.

⟰ Snowshoeing is an easy and fun family adventure

⛷ Using a sledge can give you the flexibility to cover bigger distances with young children. Just make sure you wrap them up extra warm

CROSS-COUNTRY SKIING

Cross-country skiing (also known as Nordic skiing) is generally practised on flatter ground and can take place anywhere there is snow. Ranging from prepared tracks in ski resorts to touring across field to serious mountain touring, it's a relatively easy sport to learn (descending takes the most skill), less expensive than downhill skiing/snowboarding with no lifts or passes needed, and is possible to do while carrying young children – making it an ideal sport for all families.

Using a ski trailer or sledge, you can pull babies and young children behind you. Many ski resorts have these available to hire, or else the Thule Chariot is a popular choice as it transfers to a running, off-road buggy or bike trailer for you to use the rest of the year.

Children can try cross-country skiing from a young age but you may want to continue taking a trailer or sledge with you as a back-up until you are confident they can cover the full intended distance by themselves.

THE MUIR'S GUIDE TO SKIING WITH KIDS

by Neil Muir

SKIING PROVIDES US with unmatched access to the mountains in winter, enabling us to maintain a fulfilling outdoor lifestyle throughout the darker months. The views from the top are breathtaking, and the sense of achievement and independence gained from navigating the runs from an early age cannot be underestimated.

We are a family of six who live around half an hour north of Inverness, in the Scottish Highlands. My wife, Claire, and I have both skied since we were at school. We both have fond memories of wet and windy mornings out on the hill: squeezing the water out of gloves, hats and jackets at lunchtime before heading out to do it all again in the afternoon. Skiing in the UK allows you to experience all types of snow (and rain!), and the old adage remains true: if you can ski here, you can ski anywhere.

Occasionally, the mountains clear and the winds drop. Very occasionally, this coincides with good snow. If you manage to get up on one of these special days, the memories last a lifetime (or at least they'll keep you going until the

next good day!). Perhaps the most special scenario is an inversion, when there is mist shrouding the valleys and glens; when you rise up the hill, you pop out above the clouds.

Claire and I met at university. In the years since then we have worked our way around the world and skied whenever we can, including working two winter seasons together. Skiing has given us innumerable fantastic days out and lifelong friends, and naturally, we want our children to enjoy the same opportunities.

Hamish (12) and Lottie (ten) are now competent and trustworthy enough to head out on the slopes by themselves or with their friends and cousins. The advantage of regularly skiing in the same place is that most of the staff and local skiers know them, so there is always someone on hand to help if required.

Angus (eight) and Fraser (six) enjoy chasing around after each other and are usually happy to call it a day a bit earlier and play in the snow for a while. There is always plenty of opportunity for Claire and me to squeeze in a few runs – sometimes we can even escape for a ski together.

WHEN TO GO

Skiing in the mountains of the UK is a bit more unpredictable than it once was due to rising temperatures. Snow still falls regularly between October and April each year, but it is impossible to predict when and where there will be enough to ski on. December and January see regular storms, which should bring snow,

but the accompanying gale-force winds often close uplift. February and March are safer bets, and you should still be able to ski somewhere well into April. All of the Scottish resorts have invested in modern snow-making facilities in recent years, so the availability of beginners' areas has been improved.

A common mistake is to forget about skiing until you get a dusting of snow in your garden at home. It will also have snowed on the hills, but everyone else will be breaking the skis out of the garage and heading up, so you will end up spending a lot more time in queues than you would otherwise have done. Get in the habit of checking the mountain weather forecasts and webcams: wait until there is snow on the beginners' area and then pick a dry day with light winds, particularly if going with younger children.

Take a note of the temperature on the slopes and remember that it will feel a lot colder if there is a good breeze. It will often be above freezing on the slopes, particularly in the spring, and these days can often provide the best opportunities for adventures as you'll be able to spend longer on the slopes.

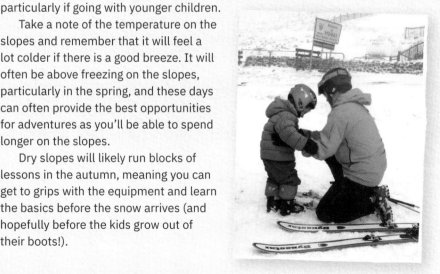

Dry slopes will likely run blocks of lessons in the autumn, meaning you can get to grips with the equipment and learn the basics before the snow arrives (and hopefully before the kids grow out of their boots!).

WHEN TO START

All our children first tried skiing shortly after they learned to walk. The first few sessions were generally very short, sometimes only a few minutes, and were just an extension of the usual snow fun of sledging and building snowmen. Certainly don't expect to spend all day outside, as you'll still have to factor in all the usual feeds, sleeps and nappy changes.

By the time they were three or four, they typically enjoyed an hour or two if we managed to time it right before they got too hungry or tired.

Every child is different, but we found that ours did not have the strength or co-ordination to stop themselves reliably before reaching five years old. Before this, we either skied down alongside them using a set of poles as a support or used a climbing harness and roof rack strap as a set of reins. (Tie the strap to the side of the harness so that you can control their hips ... if you tie it to the back, you'll just pull them over.)

Being able to use the drag lifts by themselves took another year or two. Prior to this, they can be taken up with you by leaning them against your leg, one ski on either side – check with the lift operator first. You may occasionally see people with a child between their legs ... this doesn't work on the lifts, and I've found is counterproductive when skiing down.

KEEPING MOTIVATED

You'll all be working hard, and the fresh air means hunger soon sets in. Fill your rucksack with a good stock of their favourite snacks, and dish them out liberally throughout the day. Make sure they've all had a snack and been to the toilet before they put their skis on, so you've given yourself the best start possible.

Clothing is important. Invest in a good-quality waterproof layer, as this provides the best protection from the wind as well as the wet. Use multiple layers underneath so you can put on or take off layers depending on the prevailing conditions. Be wary of wrapping up children too much, as this will just sap their energy.

Keep boots in a warm place overnight. If you leave them in a

frosty car, you'll have cold feet all of the next day. Similarly, when you're not wearing your gloves, tuck them inside your jacket. Once you have cold hands or feet, the only real remedy is to warm up inside. Take note of how you feel on the hill and time your breaks accordingly, as children will often progress to meltdown stage rather quickly.

As with most activities, most kids perform best in the company of their peers. They'll tend to make friends themselves, more often than not playing in the snow outside the cafe. Building a network of families with children of similar ages will give opportunities for them to share the learning experience and help to propel them back up the slopes.

DON'T PUT IT OFF!

Our family have all benefitted greatly from starting the kids skiing early, and I can only encourage you to seize the opportunity to do the same. Children will gain from every experience they have in the snow, and once you are up and running as a family, it opens the door to a whole world of fantastic adventures. Go for it!

CYCLING
ADVENTURES

⬍ A two-day cycling adventure from our hometown, Frome, to Bristol

OUR ADVENTURES

ON TWO WHEELS

The summer was disappearing and I was itching for a weekend adventure. I'd had in the back of my mind for a while that I wanted to try a cycle trail. So I found a route that began outside our door and finished in Bristol. It combined parts of three trails. The first was the Colliers Way, travelling through quiet country lanes and cycle trails. Then to Bath via the famous Two Tunnels path, taking you through a disused railway line and England's longest walking and cycling tunnel (Combe Down Tunnel) at over 1.6km (1 mile), before finally picking up the Bristol and Bath Railway Path.

In total, the round trip would have been 129km (80 miles), which was way too much for us to cover on our first attempt at a family cycling trip (and as beginner cyclists). So I came up with the idea that we could halve the journey by catching the train from Bath to Bristol on the first day and then from Bath to Frome on the second day. That way, we'd cover the full

≫→ Reaching our destination in Bristol

←≪ E-bikes are a great option if you don't own bikes, or are worried about fitness levels

trail without needing to double back on ourselves. Learning from forums online, I discovered Premier Inn allow you to keep bikes in your room overnight. We booked to stay a night in Bristol, feeling reassured that we wouldn't have to worry about the bikes if we went out.

I was still nervous, though. I wasn't cycling fit and hadn't owned a bike for years (a combination of having a small house and nowhere to store one and living on a hill!). Gil came up with the perfect solution: 'How about we do it on e-bikes?' A quick search found that our local council runs a scheme to hire e-bikes locally to reduce car usage. We booked a couple (at a bargain price), one with a child's seat … we were good to go.

WHY HAVEN'T WE DONE THIS BEFORE?

After a quick test run on our newly hired e-bikes on some quiet paths, we headed off on the trail. Gil carried Rivi (he's more confident on a bike), and I took our luggage, attached to the rail at the back of my bike using bungees. Naturally, cycling on roads was the part that made me most anxious, and there was no way of avoiding this for the first stretch of our route.

Within five minutes we'd turned down a country lane. I'd expected it to be quiet but not completely empty as this one was. We pootled along in the sun, cycling past fields and the occasional farmhouse. Although we

both had assisted bikes, we silently agreed that we were in no rush. The views were stunning, and the silence a welcome break after a busy few weeks. This was absolute bliss! I couldn't believe this beautiful route was right on my doorstep, and it'd taken me two years to discover it.

It took us about three times longer than we'd planned to reach the tunnel. This was due to a combination of a lot of potty stops, food breaks and realising that we'd need to stop and let Rivi nap on

←« »→ The Two Tunnels disused railway tunnel that connects Medford Valley and the City of Bath

a bench for a bit as she struggled to sleep slouched in her bike seat (we should have brought a neck pillow). It was also hot, so we were stopping a lot to hydrate and top up sunscreen. I don't think we would have made the distance without the e-bikes.

I felt the tunnel before I saw it. A sudden rush of icy cold air hit me. Turning the corner, I saw the entrance to the 1.6km (1 mile)-long disused railway tunnel entrance. We put on our lights and jumpers, gave Rivi a head torch (which she loved), and began the journey through the dark. It was an eerie experience, but fun passing the hikers and cyclists en route and taking in the light and sound art installation, which added to the experience.

It was much later than planned by the time we'd got the train to Bristol and then cycled to the Premier Inn. We were grateful to be able to leave the bikes in the room, enabling us to head out for a pizza and a walk along the harbour. Rivi fell asleep in the sling (a handy item that goes with us everywhere), even allowing us to stop for a drink while we soaked up the summer evening.

The next day, we returned to Bath along the disused railway paths connecting the two cities. It was a shorter distance but still enough to take us most of the day with all the toddler, coffee, park and cake stops on the way.

Back at home that night, I was brimming with contentment – the happiness that comes after knowing you've had the perfect weekend. The e-bikes had been an amazing discovery. They were really fun to use! I also loved that you could reduce the assistance if you wanted a bit more of a workout or bump it up when you get tired or just felt like whizzing along at speed.

Being on bikes gives the perfect balance of slow-paced travel, while also going fast enough to reach more interesting places in a day. They solve the problem of needing to carry so much gear when you ride as a family, and the various options when it comes to attaching children make them adaptable to any age. It didn't take us long to discover why so many families fall in love with cycling!

FAMILY CYCLING 101

The first thing you will need to decide when getting out cycling as a family is how you will transport your children. Most children are ready to learn to ride their own bike between the ages of three and a half and four and a half years. It will likely take some time before they are stable and robust enough to cover any distance. The road safety charity Brake doesn't recommend that children under ten cycle on the road.

Traffic-free cycling trails offer an excellent opportunity to get out as a young family, allowing children to cycle independently while reducing the risks. If you want to take on more challenging or longer cycle rides, using trailers, bike seats and tagalongs will give you the freedom to move to road cycling safely as a family.

Children must wear a helmet while cycling (including being transported by bike) and have strong neck control. It is recommended that you

Regular breaks for snacks and to stretch our legs were key

do not start transporting them until they are at least nine months old. For babies under nine months, the only option is to use a trailer that has a specially designed baby insert (usually usable until 9kg/20lb). It's worth weighing up the costs versus the use you'll get before your baby outgrows this attachment.

When using bike attachments for your children, always check the manufacturer details against your bike to ensure it is suitable and safe to carry the additional weight. Getting used to carrying additional weight will take time as the balance will change on your bike, so do some short practice runs before setting off. Remember that your child won't be exercising like you are, so they should be wrapped up warm against the wind and wearing good waterproofs if you think it might rain. Always ensure they are properly strapped into their harness.

⋙ A head torch provided excellent entertainment as we cycled through Two Tunnels

BIKE ATTACHMENTS

CHILD BIKE SEATS

Child bike seats are mounted to the frame of the bike, most commonly at the back, although some brands sit at the front between the adult riders' arms (usually called a shotgun seat).

Pros: The child is close to you, which is good for communicating, and the child gets a good view and might feel more like they are part of the action. **Cons:** The child is more exposed to weather; if you fall, they are high off the ground.

Age: Nine months to four years

BICYCLE TRAILERS

Trailers are attached to your bike so you can pull them behind you.

Pros: They are stable as they are low to the ground; they can take more than one child as well as additional gear; they usually have a cover to protect the child from the elements, which means you could potentially give the child a toy or book as the trailer is spacious; some brands allow you to convert your trailer into a buggy. **Cons:** They are more expensive; they're less visible to traffic (always use a safety flag with trailers); it's harder to communicate as the child sits further back; trailers are heavier, broader and more cumbersome to pull than tagalong bikes.

Age: Nine months to six years

CARGO BIKES

Cargo bikes allow you to carry heavier loads than you can typically haul, making it possible to transport multiple children. On cargo bikes, children tend to sit on a shelf behind the cyclist, in a front bucket, or strapped into a bike seat.

Pros: They can carry multiple children and are adaptable as children grow older; they allow you to sit close to the children, so communication is easy.
Cons: They're very expensive; children are exposed to the elements; cargo bikes are heavy and cumbersome.

Age: Nine months to ten years

Age: Four to nine years

TAGALONG/TRAILER BIKES

A single-wheeled trailer bike attaches to either your seat-post or a rear rack. This enables it to pivot when you are turning. Tagalongs allow the child to pedal and feel independent, although they rely on the adult bike for balance and control.

Pros: They allow you to cycle further; the child feels involved and independent; rider and child sit close together, so it's easy to communicate.
Cons: They're not as sturdy or stable as a trailer or bike seat; the child is open to the elements.

Note: It is possible to combine set-ups if you have multiple children. For example, you could have a child bike seat on your bike and a trailer attached.

⬆ Traffic-free cycle trails offer a great stress-free way to get out on a family cycle adventure

MOUNTAIN BIKING WITH CHILDREN

The easiest way to introduce a child aged two to five to mountain biking is with a front-mounted bike/shotgun seat. These kind of child seats differ from regular child bike seats as they position the child leaning forwards to hold on to your handlebars or additional attached handlebars. These don't increase your turning radius and don't add much weight, making them ideal for mountain biking.

The downside is that if there's a crash, your child will crash with you, so mountain biking with toddlers should only be done by experienced adults and on green (easy) graded tracks.

From the age of four, confident riders can start practising mountain biking on their own bike. Stick to green tracks in the beginning and position yourself so you're riding behind them.

PICKING A ROUTE

Start out on traffic-free cycle routes before you and your children are used to cycling together. National Cycle Network (www.sustrans.org.uk/national-cycle-network) is a network of signposted walking and cycling paths in the UK made up of 8,398km (5,220 miles) of traffic-free trails with the remaining 12,111km (7,519 miles) on-road. These trails are often alongside gentle canals, rivers or disused railways. Local parks and National Trust grounds are another great option for finding safe and quiet trails where you can get out as a family without worrying about cars.

Once you've built up confidence and cycling stamina, you can start looking at more challenging routes, road cycling or maybe even a multi-day cycling adventure. Most cycle trails aren't signposted, so you'll need to have a way to navigate. There are lots of apps available for phone navigation (including a cycle feature on Google Maps), so getting a mount for your phone to attach to your handlebar will make navigating easy (make sure it comes with a protective case if your phone isn't already waterproof).

TAKING THE STEP TO MULTI-DAY CYCLE TRIPS

We are lucky to have numerous long-distance cycle trails in the UK (page 209). As with most multi-day adventures, the accommodation you choose will greatly impact the planning, gear and logistics involved in organising the adventure. Using trailers and panniers will allow you to carry camping gear for the family, although bear in mind the extra weight once also accounting for hitchhiking children.

Using hotels, hostels and guesthouses can be tricky to organise as you'll need to check if they accept bikes inside or have a suitable place to store them safely overnight. On popular cycle trails, most of the accommodation will already be used to cyclists so should be willing to cater for this. Alternatively, Premier Inn have over 800 hotels in the UK and a great bike-friendly policy that allows you to bring your bike into your room for storing safely overnight.

≫→ Some hotels offer bicycle storage

Top tips for cycling with children

• **Get a handlebar bag** or bumbag for easy-to-grab items such as snacks, water or a dummy. This will save you having to get off the bike each time you get a demand!

• If your child is still napping, consider this when choosing your attachment. **Some seats and trailers have a reclining feature.** If not, you can see if your child can sleep with a neck support pillow. Otherwise, you'll need to factor in breaks while they sleep.

• **Get your kids interested in cycling young** by starting them on a balance bike. This will help them get used to wearing helmets and practising good balance.

• Your children will get colder quicker than you because they aren't working as hard, so **wrap them up in warm layers.**

• **Playing music or a story** on your phone from your pocket is a good last resort if you need to cover some distance and need a distraction because your little one is kicking off.

• **Have fun along the way** and have some silly games or distractions up your sleeve, from bike racing on quiet stretches to making up dance moves you can do on a bike!

CYCLING SAFETY

FOR FAMILIES

Surveys have shown that parents have been reluctant to cycle with their children as they're worried about safety. Accidents can be easily avoided, though, when following basic guidelines, such as the ones below. Cycle adventures really are a lot of fun for all the family, so it's worth investing in the right equipment and learning good safety so you have the confidence to get out on two wheels with your children.

Be bright and visible: Increase the chances of other road users spotting you and your children on bikes by dressing everyone in fluorescent and light-coloured clothing. Use head and tail lights. After dark, clothing should be reflective.

Wear a helmet: Children should be wearing correctly fitted helmets when cycling, and adults should lead by example by doing the same. A correctly fitted helmet should sit squarely on the head just above the eyebrows, not

↑ ⤞ Helmets are an essential bit of cycling safety kit,
no matter how short the journey

tilted back or forwards. It should be a snug fit and not obscure the eyes
or ears. Straps should be securely fastened and not twisted, with enough
room to fit two fingers between the chin and strap.

Only use good-quality bikes: Bikes, along with trailers and children's
seats, should be well-maintained, the correct size for the user and in
good condition.

Cycle training: There are lots of great schemes to encourage families and
children to cycle more, with training and safety instructions included.

Position yourself behind your child if they are riding separately: If your
child has their own bike, cycle behind them. If there are two adults, have
one in front and one behind your child.

Ride safely on roads

- **Prepare your children in advance** for road cycling, ensuring they are aware of the rules and your route, and the need to be extra vigilant.
- **Obey traffic lights** and road signs.
- **Avoid cycling on the pavement** unless it's a designated cycle path.
- **Signal clearly** (using your arms) when turning.
- **Look behind before you turn,** overtake or stop.
- **Ride in a position that allows you to see** and be seen – it is recommended to ride 1m (3.3ft) or more from the gutter when road cycling, so you are 'taking the lane'.
- **Make eye contact with other road users,** particularly at junctions, so you know they've seen you.
- **It's the law to have a working white front light** and red backlight, and a red rear reflector when riding at night.
- **Watch out for car doors opening** suddenly when passing parked cars.
- **Be considerate of walkers,** wheelchair users and horse riders if on a shared trail. Don't go too fast, use your bell if approaching someone, give way to others and keep left.

BIKE-PACKING BROWN KNOWE

by Trevor Worsey

....

@trevworsey

'I'VE GOT AN IDEA; let's go bike-packing together?!' If you've experienced the carnage of toddler bedtime then you will probably be spitting your coffee out right now with laughter. It's true – introducing a motivated toddler into the confines of a small bike-packing tent is a bit like trying to contain an exploding star within a wheelie bin. However, I will maintain that bike-packing can be the perfect family adventure.

First, let's get one thing straight. My wife and I are not grizzled adventurers. I have a beard, but I haven't had to fight off a bear with a Spork. My wife has never been forced to drink her own pee, and we have never slept in a drainage ditch. We are not hardcore. We just like cycling, and we like going on adventures, especially bike-packing. We also happen to be parents.

We had to hit pause on the freedom, spontaneity and dehydrated meals for a while after becoming parents. As I embarked on the white-knuckle roller coaster #dadlife journey, the one constant was and is a desire to instil in my child a love for bikes and the outdoors, that same joy that has given me so many memorable experiences. Over

the last few years, we've been on many riding adventures with our son, Brook, using a purpose-built trailer and now a front-mounted seat. Sometimes it's as simple as his daily pedal to nursery, while at other times it's a fun blast around our local trail centre or short night ride. Whichever it is, it's always been fun to immerse him in our passion.

When Brook was three, we attempted our first family bike-packing trip. The goal was simple: to introduce Brook to the wonders of cycling and sleeping under canvas, waking to the sound of birds, stiff necks and the unforgettable musky aroma of a tent full of people.

FAST AND CLOSE TO HOME

A simple plan deserves simple execution, and we intended to keep our first bike-packing adventure light and fast and close to home. We were delighted that our boy's beloved centrally mounted Kids Ride Shotgun Kids MTB Seat allowed us to fit our tried-and-tested bar and tail bag combos.

Experience has shown us that the key to successful bike-packing is carrying only the basics, barely enough to sustain life, and of course, ample wine. As such, it was a little alarming to see how many extra items we needed to accommodate the toddler. After a quick consultation with Brook, he confirmed that storybooks, Mr Bear and a toy digger were essential and could not be left behind. An hour of Tetris-style packing later, our wagon train rolled out.

I'm not going to lie: the 10km (6.2-mile) uphill ride to the summit of Brown Knowe, our local hill in the Tweed Valley, was not easy. While I love our shotgun rides, the laden bar bag and tail bag, combined with an extra 15kg (33lb) of toddler, certainly put some meat into my lactic acid sandwich. Still, as always, my loquacious co-pilot provided an excited commentary from the front seat. 'What's that, daddy?' 'Why's that, daddy?' 'Go faster, daddy!'

Finally, rolling on to the summit plateau, we scouted for 2m (6.6ft) of flat ground in the pockmarked hill. The tent was quickly pitched with 'help' from the tiny camper, and the stove fired up. The night's menu was vegetarian sausages and pasta, by no means gourmet but eaten in the context of the summit ballroom, it was a feast rivalling that of any Michelin-starred restaurant.

As the sun dipped lower, we sat back and enjoyed watching our three-year-old released into the wild. Freed from screens and noisy toys, he effortlessly

adapted to his new world, and the wide-open space became his playground to run free and explore. We chased dandelion seeds borne on the wind, shouted crap jokes at unimpressed sheep, and finally settled in the warmth of our sleeping bags as the sun wrapped us in gold.

If I said it was the best night's sleep I ever had, I would be lying. The boy claimed his spot in the tent (which turned out to be a much larger area than we were anticipating) and slept like a log. Our slumber, however, was punctuated by his relentless wriggling and the occasional lazy punch to my face. But we didn't care. It meant that we were awake to enjoy the majesty of the sunrise in peace, broken only by the occasional ripping fart from within the canvas.

Later that morning, as we sipped bitter instant coffee, the boy emerged, dressed with that iconic 'I've been camping' face, desperately seeking his own breakfast hit of warm milk and an oat pancake. We packed up and began the journey home. As we glided downhill to the house, it went quiet for a minute in the front seat, and then I heard a single sentence, not yelled but uttered quietly and genuinely: 'I love camping, daddy.'

BETTER CONNECTION

As a bike-mad family, I often reflect on how times and our objectives have changed. It's no longer about pushing ourselves to our limits or dipping our toes into the extreme. Instead, it's about taking on the challenge of doing it as a family, spending that quality time together and sharing our passions. Our family adventures have grown with our confidence and abilities, even leading us to do a bigger bike-packing adventure in New Zealand.

To other families out there, if this has ignited a flame of interest, then I would say get out there and try it. Take it steady and learn what works for your family squad. As parents, given the right tools, like a shotgun seat and some good bike-packing bags, it's possible to create a microadventure anywhere. It doesn't have to be epic; it doesn't have to be type-two fun that requires a few months for your sense of humour to recover. Seeing our boy point to the top of the local hill after a descent, an Everest to him, and saying 'We camped there!' is enough for me. Adventures are often found on your doorstep, and with a can-do attitude can be far more accessible than you think.

In truth, at his age, he will probably remember nothing of these trips, but maybe some unconscious foundations will be laid. I hope that we are building memories that will later help solidify pillars of confidence and self-belief, the idea that anything is possible and experiences are the essence of happiness. And although he won't remember them, to my wife and I, the experience is timeless. Free from the distractions of a house to tidy or a dishwasher to load, we immerse ourselves in the many excited conversations, perceptive questions and hilarious moments, strengthening the bond that binds the three of us. While there is rarely Wi-Fi at our camp spots, we have never experienced a better connection.

Adventuring together

CYCLE-TOURING ACROSS BRITTANY

by Alice Somerset and Dave Pearson-Smith

The families	The Somerset family:	The Pearson-Smith family:
	Alice	Dave
	Dave	Helen
	Agnes (aged five)	Barney (aged four)
	Winifred (aged one)	Rowan (aged two)

ALICE: Prior to children, Dave and I had always been up for an adventure. My husband is an adrenaline junky, always on the hunt for his next hit. I am more of an endorphin addict, forever on the hunt for the next exercise challenge.

Shortly after having our second daughter, we invested in a cargo bike to get us around Bristol, which quickly revolutionised our life in a big city. Both girls loved being on the bike, and I often found myself going to clear my head with both children in tow, coming back with us all feeling refreshed.

This got us thinking about a longer adventure with both children and how we could make it enjoyable for all involved. We decided that going with another family with similar-aged children would make it more fun and manageable. We had the perfect friends to do it with: the Pearson-Smith family. Agnes and

Barney get on really well and often spend hours playing together in their own little world. Winifred and Rowan have more of a love/hate relationship, which we hope will mellow with age.

The fact that all the children were similar ages meant we had a similar agenda. I think choosing the ideal people to do this trip with was one of the keys to its success.

DAVE P-S: Helen and I have been cyclists ever since we met. I grew up mountain biking every spare minute I got, whereas Helen came to it slightly later in life but made up for the lost time by cycling to Paris and then pedalling everywhere she could after that. In her younger days, she was known for having a relaxed attitude to safety: a bemused police officer once fined her for cycling through the rain with a raised umbrella in one hand!

Our earliest adventure by bike together was cycling from Berlin to Copenhagen on single-speed bikes, with a big, clunky tent and a very small budget. It was a game-changer and we made time for it as often as we could after that, until children came along and, as is tradition, put a damper on

CYCLE-TOURING ACROSS BRITTANY

everything we had found fun. Then we discovered the many and various ways you can carry children on bikes – trailers, child seats, towalongs – and the world of cycling opened up again.

When Alice and the other Dave suggested a bike-based adventure together, we had no hesitation in agreeing. Two blissful weeks of cycling, camping, swimming in the sea and spending time with our friends – what could possibly go wrong?

LUXURY IS SOMETIMES ESSENTIAL

ALICE: There was some discussion about whether we should use our e-cargo bikes or just regular bikes. We decided that regular bikes, although harder work, would feel more like an adventure and would have less potential to go wrong. After a lot of consideration and many different suggestions – from Norway to Portugal – we settled on a two-week out-and-back trip along the coast of Brittany in western France. This, we decided, would give the perfect blend of being abroad, great cycling and accessibility.

We booked a ferry from Plymouth to Roscoff in August with the plan to cycle on and off the ferry on both sides. We'd done some research and learned that there were some amazing, very well-signposted cycle routes throughout

Bike set-up

Somerset's bike set-up:
• 1 x adult bike with Yepp Nexxt Mini child seat and Single Croozer Trailer attached
• 1 x adult bike with FollowMe tandem for a 50cm (20in) child's bike

Pearson-Smith's bike set-up:
• 1 x adult bike with Hamax Siesta child seat and Burley Bee double trailer attached
• 1 x adult bike with a shotgun saddle seat

Europe, one of which, the EuroVelo 4 (EV4), went through Roscoff. That left us eight months of discussions around logistics and planning to work out kit, schedules and how to safely and comfortably transport all the children.

Helen and Dave weighed their bikes fully loaded. The bikes with trailer, racks, panniers, clothes, camping gear, toys, children and riders sat squarely in the super-heavyweight category: Helen's rig was a hefty 160kg (25st 3lb) all in and Dave P-S's a colossal 210kg (33st 1lb). We were all going to have serious calves by the end of the trip for sure!

Most of the time, our bike set-up was as follows, although there was a lot of flexibility, allowing us to change things up depending on the mood. Sometimes the older kids would ride separately on their bikes for short spells and could switch between the trailers, riding tandem or being in a shotgun seat.

Before the trip, we did a 'dry run' overnighter in Wales with all our gear (which turned out to be an exceptionally wet run). This was helpful for working out what would be essential for the trip and what could be left behind. One discovery was that a huge tarpaulin would be a necessary bit of kit to allow us all to gather together and cook at the end of the day, regardless of the weather. This became Dave P-S's favourite thing and he took great pride in building us the perfect shelter at every campsite.

Another luxury was camping chairs for the adults (adding a combined 6kg/13lb). We repeatedly said every evening when sitting under the tarp on our comfy chairs with a beer in hand that these had been our two best ideas!

Before we knew it, we were on the ferry and feeling a mixture of excitement and nerves. We were finally starting our planned cycle route, kicking off with a very short day and a close-by campsite where Dave P-S set about putting up his first tarp of the trip (I'd grade this particular one at least a seven out of ten).

UNDERWAY IN FRANCE

DAVE P-S: Once we were properly underway, we began to settle into a daily rhythm: pack up early in the morning, eat an ill-advisedly large quantity of baguettes and croissants, squeeze into our padded shorts and hit the road at the crack of mid-morning. The kids loved hanging out with us on the bikes – they had our undivided attention, and there is no closeness like that found when you are balanced 15cm (6in) apart on two wheels with the wind whistling in your ears. We pointed out ancient Breton churches, played I Spy and invented pretend French words for the things we saw. Most of our route remained close to the coast, and we had frequent and lingering views of the sun shimmering across the waves and cormorants drying themselves on the rocks (or were they eagles – who knows?).

Whenever the kids wanted to stop, we stopped; there is a reason people call cycling 'slow travel' and that is never truer than with four kids on board. There was always at least one child who needed something, whether a snack,

a nappy change or to pick up an especially appealing stick they had noticed about half a mile back and just now remembered. However, ultimately, we discovered that children, who everyone knows are endlessly demanding and infuriating, are also able to relax into the freedom of cycling. They spent long periods of time quietly admiring the views or singing mangled versions of children's songs (I taught the eldest two 'Frère Jacques', and quickly wished I hadn't as we heard nothing else for at least an hour).

We had finished the practice ride in Wales tired, grumpy and concerned that two weeks of this might finish our marriages or our friendship. Now that worry had turned to a sense of optimism that this might actually be the joyful adventure we had always hoped it would be.

THEN THINGS DIDN'T EXACTLY START GOING TO PLAN

ALICE: The difficulties started to creep up on us a few days into the ride. The kids began to tire of sitting still for so long each day, our legs began to tire of the battle against gradient and weight, and all of us began to tire of having to reach a distant goal each day. The kids were becoming tetchy, the adults downright fractious, and the wheels were beginning to fall off our big adventure. We realised there was a danger that none of us would be enjoying this if we carried on as we were.

Then came the revelation: we could just stop. We didn't have to cycle 40 or more very hilly kilometres each day with heavy loads and needy children. We could just pitch camp at a nice spot and stay there until everyone was ready to move on again. Everyone could get some rest and enjoy the sunshine on the beach, and when we all felt refreshed, we could set off the next morning with strong legs.

I think this is what turned our trip from a slog into an adventure. By the time we had spent two nights in one place, the kids were ready to see the next port on our voyage, and the adults were ready to turn the pedals again. The difficulty of dragging nearly a quarter of a tonne up a steep, roughly tarmacked hill with a crying child on the back is not to be taken lightly, but once you are on the other side of a beer and a reasonable night's sleep, things look a little different.

Once we had settled into this pace of life, new possibilities opened up. Possibly the highlight of the whole trip was when, while floating breathlessly down a hill after the most strenuous climb on the route, we suddenly happened across what was understatedly signposted as a 'Food Truck' but turned out to be a global street food-inspired pop-up cafe, complete with yurts, decking and a live band. While Helen lifted a sleeping Rowan off her bike and laid him in the shade, the rest of us drooled over the fried rice, curries and *moules-frites*.

CYCLE OUT, CYCLE BACK

DAVE P-S: Brittany is a fantastic place to travel by bike with children, once we had agreed to stick to the marked cycle routes (ie I had shouted very rudely at the other Dave for navigating us on to a main road to mix in with the lorries and then had to stammer a shamefaced apology a few minutes later when we arrived at a stunning estuary with the perfect place for a picnic). Everyone has a different view of risk and that is perhaps even more true among parents, but for us this ride represented the sweet spot of safe adventure with children. The idea of two weeks without beds, TV screens or a microwave might fill some parents with horror, but it is amazing how resilient and adaptable kids are; within hours, shoes were eschewed in favour of dirty feet and Paw Patrol was a distant memory.

Our route plan was simple: once we had cycled for nearly a week, we would turn around and pedal back to the ferry. Any concerns about this making the

ride repetitive soon dissolved as all the climbs we had conquered became descents, and we enjoyed new views of the places we had already been. On the way out we had spotted some beautiful campsites so we visited them on the return leg, and they didn't disappoint. A particular highlight was one pitch only a few yards from an enormous sandy white beach, where we could fly kites and swim in the day and supervise sleeping children in their tents in the evening with a beer and the sea lapping at our feet. Even the fearsome wind that blew up one night didn't faze us by this point, especially with some judicious tarp pitching (an eight out of ten, this one, I reckon).

TIME TO HEAD HOME

ALICE: The penultimate leg of the ride ended on the spot where we first pitched camp – a granite-studded peninsula that had been surrounded by glassy, translucent water on our arrival a couple of weeks before. Now it was black and foam-flecked; the wind had picked up, and the rain began in earnest.

Nearly two weeks of pedalling big rigs were beginning to take their toll and small injuries were creeping in. We are all regular cyclists, but for those with less experience or fitness, I would recommend choosing as flat a route as possible when planning a cycling adventure with children.

On top of that, Rowan had succumbed to some kind of virus and looked very ropey, and even Agnes and Barney were beginning to fall out. We had loved every minute of our adventure, but it felt like the right time to call it a day.

DAVE P-S: The next morning, with the skies still looking ominous, we packed down for the final time and pedalled slowly back to the ferry, drinking in the views one last time. As we strapped our bikes on to the deck and headed up the stairs to the lounge, I reflected that this was the first time I had been properly inside for two weeks. I felt ready to return to civilisation and our regular routines, but I suddenly felt a tinge of longing for life on the road. There's only one solution, really: we'll have to do it all again.

ALICE: Maybe the year after next, though, yes?

The Somerset family packing list
(for two adults and two children)

Sleeping:
- 2 x small two-man tents
- 4 x sleeping mats
- 4 x sleeping bags
(Winnie's was just a baby one)
- blow-up pillows
(our Alpkit ones were great)
- tarp
- 2 x camping chairs

General:
- waterproofs, warm clothes, spare clothes and cycling shorts
- 3 x headtorches
- European travel plug, battery pack and spare batteries
- toiletries: hairbrush and ties, hair and body wash, toothbrush and paste
- well-stocked first aid kit and any medication
- swimming costumes and camping towels
- dry bags to separate items

Cooking:
- kitchen bits: tea towels, scourer, washing-up liquid, bin bags
- washing line, pegs and powder
- small Alpkit Koro stove and 2 x Trangia pans
- gas and lighter
- 4 x bowls, 3 x mugs, sippy cup for Winnie
- 4 x sets of cutlery
- 3 x water bottles and 2 x 2L hydration packs (attached to frame bags on bikes)

Bike-related:
- 4 x helmets
- puncture repair kit, pump and bike tools
- 4 x bike locks
- bike lights
- passport and euros

TRAFFIC-FREE
CYCLE TRAILS

Try out some of the UK's most popular and picturesque trails. These are either entirely or mostly traffic-free, with any road cycling kept to short distances on quiet country roads. Some of the longer trails could be split into multi-day adventures.

TARKA TRAIL, ENGLAND
(48KM/30 MILES)

This is one of England's longest traffic-free cycle paths. Using disused railway tracks, the trail offers beautiful views of North Devon. Sculptors have designed benches and shelters on the trail, making for great pit stops.

BRISTOL AND BATH
RAILWAY TRAIL, ENGLAND
(21KM/13 MILES)

This route connects these two very different bike-friendly cities. Along the way, you can find a variety of sculptures and also a working steam engine at Bitton. Stop for a pub lunch at Saltford. When you

The Tarka Trail, Instow

reach Bath, you can tag on the Combe Down Tunnel. At over 1.6km (1 mile) in length, this is the UK's longest walking and cycling tunnel. Going through the tunnel is a memorable experience, heightened by an audio-visual installation.

➤➤ The Bristol and Bath Railway Trail

LAGAN AND LOUGH CYCLE WAY, NORTHERN IRELAND (32KM/20 MILES)

Travel from Lisburn to Jordanstown via Belfast. A mix of canal and river side, park paths and city centre cycling. You will find lots of artwork en route commissioned by local sculptor artists.

PEREGRINE PATH, WALES (12KM/7.5 MILES)

Follow the stunning River Wye, hugging the England–Wales border, on this short and mostly traffic-free cycle trail. Beginning in the historic market town of Monmouth, the trail meanders along the river past Symonds Yat East and The Kymin – the perfect picnic spot offering views across Wales.

MAWDDACH TRAIL, WALES (14.5KM/9 MILES)

Travelling from Dolgellau to Barmouth, this short but beautiful route runs along the Mawddach Estuary below the foothills of Cader Idris. The area is rich with birdlife.

⚓ Mawddach Estuary on the Mawddach Trail

⚑ The Camel Trail, Cornwall

CAMEL TRAIL, ENGLAND (19KM/12 MILES)

A popular trail for cyclists in Cornwall, this flat route follows an old railway line, running from Padstow to Poley's Bridge. With woodland, moorland and an estuary, you can expect a varied and interesting ride.

EXE ESTUARY TRAIL, ENGLAND (37KM/23 MILES)

This is a flat cycle trail along both sides of Devon's Exe Estuary. Expect fantastic views and a lot of wildlife spotting as the marshes are a haven for birds. The pretty villages of Topsham and Exton provide great hot chocolate and lunch stops. To turn the ride into a loop, catch the Starcross ferry to the west of the estuary when you reach Exmouth.

THE UNION AND FORTH & CLYDE CANALS, SCOTLAND (90KM/56 MILES)

Running from Edinburgh to Glasgow this is an impressive traffic-free trail, perfect for families looking for a longer cycling adventure. The trail runs along the Union Canal towpath, a sanctuary for wildlife. You'll also pass the famous Falkirk Wheel, the rotating boat lift.

⚑ Falkirk Wheel along the Union and Forth & Clyde Ca

THREE PARKS TRAIL, WALES
(21KM/13 MILES)

This path takes in three of Wales' parks – Sirhowy Valley Country Park, Parc Penallta and Parc Taf Bargoed – and is a part of the longer Celtic Trail. Look out for 'The Wheel of Drams', an 8m (26ft)-tall landmark, and the Sulan the Pit Pony figurative earth sculpture. The path also passes Trelewis Climbing Centre where you can take part in a number of outdoor activities including indoor climbing and kayaking.

CONSETT AND SUNDERLAND RAILWAY PATH, ENGLAND
(39KM/24 MILES)

Following a disused railway line in Tyne and Wear, this trail meanders alongside the river and through the marina. It ends at the beach in Roker. En route, you'll spot specially commissioned artwork as well as an open-air museum.

DERBY CANAL PATH AND CLOUD TRAIL, ENGLAND
(21KM/13 MILES)

A journey along canal paths and disused railways, this trail runs from Derby city centre to Worthington. You will pass the Trent Viaduct near the picturesque town of Melbourne. From Cloud Quarry, there's an option to extend your ride for another 16km (10 miles) along quiet lanes and traffic-free trails to reach Loughborough.

LONDON DOCKLANDS AND LEA VALLEY, ENGLAND
(34KM/21 MILES)

Travel through the Isle of Dogs then follow the Regent's Canal and the River Lea. This trail passes many iconic attractions including the *Cutty Sark*, Mudchute Park and Farm, Victoria Park and Queen Elizabeth Olympic Park.

COMBER GREENWAY, NORTHERN IRELAND
(11KM/7 MILES)

A short and peaceful cycle path from Comber to the heart of East Belfast. The route is a haven for wildlife and offers views of Stormont, Scrabo Tower, the Harland & Wolff cranes and the Belfast Hills. Near the end of the trail, you will pass the CS Lewis statue at the Holywood Arches.

CUCKOO TRAIL, ENGLAND
(18KM/11 MILES)

This popular family-friendly East Sussex cycle trail passes woodland, open grassland and pasture. Look out for green woodpeckers on the trail, as well as oak sculptures and carved wooden seats.

STRATHKELVIN RAILWAY PATH, SCOTLAND
(13KM/8 MILES)

Cycle on disused railway lines from Kirkintilloch and Strathblane. An easy and surfaced trail, expect beautiful views of the Campsie Fells and the Strathblane Hills.

NEWRY CANAL TOWPATH, NORTHERN IRELAND (32KM/20 MILES)

A cycle route following the bank of the former Newry Canal, starting from Portadown and ending in Newry Town Hall. Scarva Visitor Centre is close to the trail and makes for a good place to break.

SWISS VALLEY CYCLE ROUTE, WALES (18KM/11 MILES)

Following a disused railway line into rural woodland, this route is a gentle climb, offering glimpses of the Lliedi Reservoirs and views across the Gwendraeth Valley.

BLACKPOOL TO FLEETWOOD, ENGLAND (14.5KM/9 MILES)

The promenade quickly leads you from the bustle of Blackpool to quiet stretches of the Fylde coast. There are lots of places to stop for chips, ice cream or a dip in the sea. On a clear day, you can see the Isle of Man.

CARDIFF TO CASTELL COCH, WALES (14.5KM/9 MILES)

Starting in Bute Park and finishing in Castell Coch, this route follows the River Taff through the heart of the city. You'll pass Melingriffith Water Pump, a water-powered beam engine built in 1807 to lift water 3.4m (11ft) from the river to the Glamorganshire Canal.

Castell Coch, Cardiff

LONG-DISTANCE
CYCLE TRAILS

If you are ready for a bigger challenge, it might be time to tackle a long-distance cycle trail. These trails involve cycling on roads across varied terrain and carrying additional gear for overnight camping or accommodation. They should, therefore, only be attempted by experienced cyclists who are confident taking children cycling on roads.

Although logistics, weather and achy legs will make for a challenge, the views, slow travel and freedom will make up for the hard work – leaving lasting memories for all the family.

COAST TO COAST, ENGLAND
(306KM, 3,410M/190 MILES, 11,188FT)

44.6 per cent traffic-free | 83.8 per cent asphalt, 14.3 per cent unsealed firm, 1.8 per cent unsealed loose

The C2C is the UK's most popular cycle route. Starting at the Irish sea in the west, the route travels the width of northern England before finishing at the North Sea in the east. The C2C is a mix of on-road and off-road (although the route can be alternated to be fully on-road). This challenge takes you through the stunning Lake District National Park. This is a very hilly route so is only suitable for those able to manage long, steep climbs with their children.

CALEDONIAN WAY, SCOTLAND (377KM, 540M/234 MILES, 1,772FT)

26.7 per cent traffic-free | 85.1 per cent asphalt, 11.5 per cent unsealed firm, 3.5 per cent unsealed loose

This takes you through breathtaking scenery and plenty of lochs and mountains before ending at Inverness in the Scottish Highlands. It combines quiet country roads with traffic-free trails and gravel sections so you'll need a mountain bike. This moderate trail is a great challenge for a family looking for wilderness and wild camping.

SOUTH DOWNS WAY, ENGLAND (160KM, 4,150M/ 100 MILES, 13,616FT)

75.7 per cent traffic-free | 58.0 per cent unsealed firm, 28.7 per cent asphalt, 13.3 per cent unsealed loose

Mainly an off-road mountain bike route, the SDW takes you through woodlands and rolling hills. Although the endless hilly climbs shouldn't be underestimated, the tracks are gentle and the cafe and pub stops plentiful, making this a good choice for a family cycling adventure.

HADRIAN'S CYCLEWAY, ENGLAND (274KM, 1,490M/ 170 MILES, 4,889FT)

32.2 per cent traffic-free | 97.7 per cent asphalt, 1.2 per cent unsealed loose, 1.1 per cent unsealed firm

Take a journey through the history of Ancient Britain in a World Heritage Site. This route cruises from village to village, following the line of the 2,000-year-old Hadrian's Wall. It is a great adventure for families with coastal views, sweeping hills, Roman forts, museums and quaint villages. All bikes are suitable. The terrain is a mixture of on-road and traffic-free sections and relatively flat, with a few steep sharp sections in the middle.

NORTH COAST 500, SCOTLAND (800KM, 10,000M/ 500 MILES, 32,808FT)

100 per cent asphalt

A challenging cycle ride alongside an equally popular driving route, but a true adventure with impressive scenery, the NC500 is often dubbed Scotland's answer to Route 66. You'll be cycling through remote wild places perfect for wild camping, although there are plenty of hotels and guesthouses if you prefer. Challenges will include midges, Scotland's notorious weather, sharing the road with inexperienced visiting drivers, and a whopping 10,000m (32,808ft) of elevation gain. This is not a challenge for the faint-hearted!

YORKSHIRE WOLDS, ENGLAND (232KM, 2,160M/144 MILES, 7,087FT)

5.8 per cent traffic-free | 99.1 per cent asphalt, 0.6 per cent unsealed firm, 0.3 per cent unsealed loose

This circular route offers chalkland hills and picturesque English countryside. Passing through small villages, market towns and seaside Bridlington, pit stops are plentiful. There are also country houses, nature reserves, historical sites and landmarks to be admired for cyclists who have time on their side. The Yorkshire Wolds is best ridden in a clockwise direction. With trains running to Beverley and Malton, these both make good starting points.

LÔN LAS CYMRU (224KM, 5,700M/139 MILES, 18,700FT)

28.9 per cent traffic-free | 98.8 per cent asphalt, 0.8 per cent unsealed firm, 0.4 per cent unsealed loose

Cutting through the heart of Wales, this route visits both of the countries' national parks – Snowdonia and Bannau Brycheiniog/the Brecon Beacons. The Lôn Las Cymru travels from Cardiff to Holyhead, visiting some of the most scenic parts of Wales. This is not an easy cycle route and features lots of big and steep climbs.

Still not epic enough for you? Then how about taking on the iconic LEJOG (Land's End to John o'Groats), a 1,641km (1,020 mile)-long cycle route the length of mainland UK. Or the massive 2,575km (1,600 mile)-long Wild Atlantic Way, which winds itself all around the Irish west coast and is one of the longest coastal routes in the world!

Kylesku Bridge, along the NC500

CYCLE-TOURING THE HEBRIDEAN WAY

by Rachel Healey

@purplecavingcat_adventures | YouTube: @adventuretraveller007

I WAS LUCKY as a child that I was born into an adventurous family with adventurous parents and grandparents. It is perhaps no surprise then that when I had kids of my own, I had grand plans...

However, when we had three kids in four years, those plans moderated somewhat, and although we lived an active and outdoor lifestyle, we definitely weren't adventuring quite how I'd imagined we might. It turns out that adventuring with multiple small kids is actually fairly complicated, and we found ourselves facing various barriers to the lifestyle we really wanted to live. Predominantly, those were cost (we chose to be a single-income family with me at home raising the kids), the endless nappies, the lack of sleep and the biggest thing of all – how DO you carry all the kit AND the kids? Undeterred, we started to try to find a way, and initially, the way we found was in canoes.

TESTING THE WATERS WITH FAMILY ADVENTURES

My husband, Ian, and I were already competent expedition canoeists; before kids, we'd taken canoe journeys in Scotland and Alaska. Turning to canoes made sense to us – with a canoe you can carry all the kit, even if it's big, heavy

and not that well suited to being carried – which ours wasn't because 'good' lightweight kit costs money, which we didn't have.

We loved those early canoe trips. Our first was two nights down the River Wye when the boys were aged three, five and seven, and canoeing quickly proved itself to be a perfect vehicle for family adventures – it's easy to carry lots of heavy (cheap) kit and the children didn't need to do anything if they didn't want to (we paddled with rafted boats while the

kids played, snoozed or threw sticks and stones into the water!).

The following winter, I spent hours and hours researching lighter and smaller equipment and then even more hours finding second-hand deals on the internet. Bit by bit, we gathered the kit we needed, and by spring, we were ready to try our first wild camps in the mountains. We chose spots with a short walk-in, loaded up the kids with their new rucksacks and three-quarter-length bed mats, and spent nights camping in Bannau Brycheiniog/the Brecon Beacons and the Pembrokeshire Coast. The boys loved it. But still, we couldn't quite work out how to turn these short trips into longer ones. How on earth could we carry enough food? Would we cope with days of rain? Would it still be fun? And if it wasn't fun – would there be any point in doing it?

AN UNCOMFORTABLE START TO CYCLE TOURING

As a young child, I had been cycle-touring with my own parents. The first time we went, I was about six and my brother was three. He rode on the back of my mum's bike and I had a tiny red folding bicycle that would randomly fold up as I cycled along, adding an exciting unpredictability to every trip!

I have fond memories of those adventures, and I was keen to try them with our kids. It was a couple more years though before they could ride their own bikes and we had the kit and bikes we needed. Merlin (aged nine) and Roo (aged seven) both rode their own bikes with small panniers on the back, and Sol (aged five) was on a tagalong bike being towed by Ian. Carrying all the kit still wasn't easy, but we managed it and set off on a two-day ride from Nailsea (south of Bristol) to Bradford-on-Avon.

That first trip wasn't a total disaster, but it wasn't a total success either. To say we made slow progress that first day was an understatement – by tea time, we were still in Bristol, and we had to arrange for the kind campsite host to open up the campsite again at 9pm to let us in!

On the second day we reached Freshford, 8km (5 miles) short of our target, and abandoned the trip for the comfort of a train to our final destination. We'd bitten off more than we could chew, and I was in agony – a badly fitting bike and bike seat left me unable to sit down or walk comfortably for a week afterwards.

For a couple of years, I resisted the idea of another bike trip – the butt pain had been too great to forget easily! We continued taking short overnight trips in the mountains here in the UK and in the Alps. We took more canoe trips, too, and slowly the boys grew a little bigger, and our kit grew a little lighter and smaller. Then one day, I unexpectedly inherited £500 and, on a whim, blew it all on buying myself a shiny new touring bike. Once I owned it, I just had to use it! That same winter, a new long-distance walking path was announced, running the length of the Outer Hebrides. Immediately, it caught my attention, but realistically a 320km (200-mile) walk just didn't seem possible with small kids in tow. As I browsed the internet and dreamed of visiting the islands, I discovered there was also a matching cycle route from the southern tip of Vatersay to the northern tip of Lewis and Harris. And an idea began to form in my mind...

THE HEBRIDEAN WAY

This is how we found ourselves on the quayside in Oban with five bikes, 12 panniers and three kids (now aged 12, 10 and 8), anxiously waiting to catch the ferry to Barra. The preparation had taken me literally months – I'd identified the location of every food shop on the islands (not many, as it turns out), planned and replanned daily distances and packed and repacked our panniers over and over. There'd been new clothing to buy because the kids kept growing, and hanging over me the whole time was the huge unknown – could we actually manage this?

We'd planned a 10- to 12-day trip – at least eight days longer than any other trip we'd done. I'd read about other families who had undertaken huge trips, but could we do it or were these other families somehow stronger, braver, fitter or more skilled than we could ever be? There is, in the end, only one way to find out...

Looking back, the Outer Hebrides was the perfect place for our first long trip. We were all beguiled by the landscape. The beautiful golden sand beaches, the machair and the rolling bleak moorland, dotted with tiny thatched crofts. The birdlife was incredible, and although we never saw an otter, we kept trying. The island's motorists are easily the friendliest I've ever met in the UK, and only twice did I ever feel slightly unsafe on the roads out there, despite them being

so narrow that cars were often waiting some time for us to find a safe place for them to pass us.

We wild camped on all but two nights, and the Right to Roam laws in Scotland made that a breeze. We'd planned to ride roughly 32km (20 miles) each day, which proved a good distance for us, allowing plenty of time for resting, chilling out in camp, shopping and visiting some of the sites we passed. We were cold at times, so we drank a LOT of hot drinks and ran out of gas for our stove as a result (thankfully, we found more in a farm supply shop).

As we'd predicted, the shopping wasn't easy – you certainly can't find handy freeze-dried camping meals in the tiny village shops, so we ate a lot of baked beans, pasta and pesto, and instant mash. We had anticipated having more meals out than we managed – there really aren't many places to eat out, and our low daily mileage meant that at times we were spending several days without passing as much as a shop.

The smaller southern islands of the Outer Hebrides were undoubtedly my favourites. Most of the islands are connected by causeways, with two ferries between Barra and Eriskay, and Berneray and Harris. Many of the islands are low-lying, peppered with lochans and scoured by the wind. We were very lucky with the weather. We had one night of rain, one hard frost and two days of streaming, strength-sapping wind, but we also had beautiful sunshine and came home from our Easter holiday with a tan.

BUMPS IN THE ROAD

We had a couple of breakdowns, and I would *strongly* advise anybody setting off on a cycle journey with kids to learn how to carry out basic repairs before you go (mending punctures, changing broken spokes and chains, adjusting brakes and indexing gears). Moving bikes to a repair shop if you cannot ride them is complicated and expensive at best (and impossible at worst!).

On this trip, when we reached Eriskay, Merlin snapped his chain as we set off from the ferry, and while trying to fix it, Ian broke our only chain tool (facepalm!). Locals flooded to help, and eventually (and luckily) we found another chain tool on the tiny island and botched a repair. The next day and 20 odd miles north on South Uist, we got it fixed properly at one of the only bike repair shops in the area – we were lucky it happened where it did.

Roo also managed to break a spoke on his bike. We've broken at least one spoke on every subsequent tour we've undertaken – kids ride their (heavily loaded) bikes hard and bounce them off curbs without a care in the world – beware!

Vatersay, Barra, Eriskay, South Uist, Benbecula, Grimsay, North Uist and Berneray all passed far too quickly. The riding was smooth and predominantly flat(ish). Lewis and Harris felt very different. Our first full day on Harris involved crossing a smallish mountain pass; the wind was howling, making us all feel the cold. We'd been wild camping for five nights and had promised ourselves a rare night in a hostel when we reached Tarbert – our budget doesn't stretch to indoor accommodation very easily.

We genuinely hadn't expected the hostel to be full – it was after all only early April and the islands felt very quiet. But the hostel receptionist was adamant that they could *not* fit us in. I was devastated and had to hold back genuine tears of grief for the hot shower I'd been dreaming of all day. We regrouped on the town green and ate a whole packet of biscuits while we decided what to do. The ferry to Skye was sitting there in the harbour, calling to me. It was my personal low point of the trip – the temptation to jump on the ferry and head home to a hot shower and comfortable bed was strong. Ian was trying to talk me out of it, and the kids were clearly sorely tempted by the lure of Wi-Fi and phone chargers.

Suddenly the receptionist from the hostel appeared – she'd chatted with the other residents, and they were happy for the boys to join me in the women's dorm. She'd made space for us. As I type this, the memory of her kindness still brings tears to my eyes. The ferry blasted its horn and left the island, and we headed inside for hot showers, Wi-Fi, phone charging and oven pizzas... Bliss!

The next day, we took time off the bikes, visited the island distillery and rode a paltry 4.8km (3 miles) to our camp spot in the evening.

Lewis has an entirely different feeling to the rest of the islands. It's large, and mountainous enough to feel less like an island. The roads are bigger and busier and the cycle route moves away from the coast for a large part of the island's length. If we did the trip again, I would skip Lewis and take the ferry back to Skye, but on this trip I'm really glad we didn't. The accomplishment of pushing past the hard bits and reaching the Butt of Lewis Lighthouse on the northern tip of the Outer Hebrides was indescribable. The Butt of Lewis makes an amazing end point as the land drops into the ocean. We'd reached the end.

We celebrated by shaking and spraying a huge bottle of Coke all over each other (champagne is so last year!) and lifted our bikes over our heads to prove our strength to the world – I had no idea I was strong enough – and yet it turns out I was!

DEFINING WHO WE ARE AS A FAMILY

That evening, we camped by the most incredible little cove, and we all took the shortest and coldest sea swim ever. Ian and I shared a very tiny bottle of Prosecco as the sun set and the boys played in the sand.

The following morning, we were picked up by a bike-compatible taxi company to shuttle us back to Stornoway for the ferry back to the mainland, followed by a complicated and tortuous bus journey for Ian back to Oban to retrieve our vehicle.

Our first foray into longer human-powered journeys was so successful and rewarding that we have carried on adventuring with the kids. Later that year, we undertook another ten-day cycle tour in France, and in the autumn, we paddled the Great Glen Canoe Trail. In the following years we've cycled the Devon Coast to Coast and walked the West Highland Way (our first long hiking trip). We've cycled the Coast and Castles route from Newcastle to Aberdeen over 18 days, undertaken a second Scottish canoe expedition and, our biggest adventure yet, spent 40 days cycling from Portsmouth to Spain – 1,288km (800 miles) of riding along the Vélodyssée EuroVelo1 route down the French west coast.

Undertaking long and hard expeditions as a family has come to define who we are and has helped our boys grow into confident young men. Merlin is now planning his own trips – as soon as he has time among his exams and studies he plans to cycle solo to every lifeboat station in the UK. Roo is now a confident and social teenager who chats to everybody he meets and is comfortable with being uncomfortable – a skill I am still learning! Sol *knows* he can do hard things – when we reached Spain, he turned to me and said 'We did it!' He still reminds me every couple of weeks of what we achieved.

Reading an account like this, I know first-hand how easy it is to think, 'My kids aren't like that, though' and to discount family adventures as something that only other families can do. But my kids are perfectly normal – left to their own devices, they'd spend all day on their computers and never leave the house.

Adventuring helps us provide balance. Nine years after our first tentative forays into family adventures, my kids still moan, they still have days where it's all too much, and increasingly they just want to stay home and hang out with friends. When we're mid-adventure and one of them is breaking, I remind myself that we have hard times at home, too. Everybody has bad days, whether they are at home or on a remote Scottish island. But I also know now that hard is worthwhile – that's where the growth really hides.

Cruising along the Brecon and Monmouthshire Canal in our hired canal boat

WATER
ADVENTURES

OUR ADVENTURES
ON WATER

We'd lost our biggest champion. Cooper, my nephew (aged six), had been bragging for weeks to anyone who would listen that he was being taken on a cruise. In reality, we were hiring a canal boat for a mid-week break in Wales for the October half term. We'd stuck with the word 'cruise' for now, though, happy that one of the three kids we were taking was so enthused by our adventure plans, even if not entirely accurate.

Cooper's enthusiasm had plummeted with just an hour to go before we reached Llangattock, where we'd be collecting our boat from Brecon Park Boats (www.beaconparkboats.com). His constant 'Are we there yet?' enquiries had been replaced by 'I want to go home'.

'You don't want to go on the cruise? It'll be really cool! You get to steer the boat! You're going to be a pirate!' I desperately tried to get some of his earlier enthusiasm back.

'No,' he replied flatly.

The journey began to unravel. Dulcie, my niece (aged eight) kept declaring she was hungry, despite devouring three bowls of porridge and a slice of toast just an hour ago. Rivi, aged two, was angrily demanding her dummy.

'But you've got a dummy in your mouth?'

'Other dummy!' she cried back at me.

When we arrived at Brecon Park Boats, the fleet of neatly painted green boats was lined up, and the car park was a flurry of activity with holidaymakers unloading their cars and snapping pictures. We had a warm welcome and were given a large trolley to fill and load our

↑ Cooper 'fishing' from the side of the boat

↞ Picking a picturesque mooring spot, we then got stuck into cooking dinner

⥮ We hired our canal boat from Brecon Park Boats. This one was especially spacious and came with three double beds and two bathrooms

luggage before heading down to the pontoon to find our boat.

Cooper had now switched from asking every five minutes to go home to running between the boat and our car, screaming, 'I think that massive boat is ours!' ('OK, great – but stay away from the water.') Dulcie asked if she could go to the boat shop opposite the pontoon ('Yes – but don't touch anything, and we aren't buying anything!'), and Rivi was running and jumping in circles making monkey sounds. She had no idea why the excitement levels of the older kids had suddenly rocketed, but that wasn't going to stop her. ('Just hold my hand please Rivi and watch for cars!').

I think I preferred the grumpy demands. This was the part of the trip I'd been most stressed about. Before setting off, we had to unload all our stuff on to the boat, watch an instructional video on how to use the boat, get the kids fitted out with life vests and then have a short 'driving lesson'. We'd been warned it would take at least an hour, and as neither Gil nor I had driven a canal boat before, we were anxious to make sure we learned everything we needed to.

We had a plan, however. We got the kids on board and seated in the salon (practically blindfolding them on the way, so we didn't trigger the 'Which bed is mine?' debate); Gil whipped out his laptop and started playing a film. I threw a handful of snacks at them and was grateful when one of the staff members gave each of them a carton of juice.

Gil went about watching the introduction video while I unpacked our mountain of luggage. As instructed, we'd used soft bags (mostly supermarket 'bags for life') as storage on the boat was limited to small, awkward spaces. It was the first time I could take in the boat properly. It was stunning. The owner of Brecon Park Boats said the *Orient Express* had inspired the design of *Falcon*, our boat, and I could see the influence immediately with the wooden finish, brass fixtures and quaint lamps fixed to the corridor side of beds.

At the back of the boat was the tiller (for steering), and on one side, four steps (watch your head!) to take you into the belly of the boat. On the left was a long corridor (I had to stoop slightly while walking down it, although it was perfectly spacious for the kids). Three double beds

were permanently set up on the right-hand side, one after the other. They came with bedding and were already set up. Between the beds were two bathrooms (with a sink, flushing toilet and shower – hot water heated by the onboard heater or engine) and two narrow wardrobes for storage; the doors also opened to create a partition between the beds for privacy.

↯»→ Cooper gets stuck into mooring the boat

At the front of the boat was a fully equipped kitchen and, on the other side of the 'galley', two padded seating areas facing each other – in between, you could make a table appear magically or could even turn the area into a fourth bed if needed. Beyond that, two doors opened to a small outdoor space.

Throughout the boat, many windows were pouring in natural light. There were also a lot of buttons everywhere. Remote control blinds, lights, heaters, important-looking engine buttons, and even one to make a hidden TV appear in the seating area (I'm immediately dreaded the hundred times I was going to have to say 'Don't press the buttons!').

I felt excited about spending the next few days self-contained on this boat. This was awesome; I'd always dreamed of living on a boat.

Before long, we were having our very-fast driving lesson and the instructor was hopping off our boat on to the shore before waving us off. We were on our own! The boat was relatively easy to drive, chugging along at around 3.3–4km/h (2–2.5mph), using the big tiller at the back to steer. Still, we both felt anxious that we'd been left alone so quickly. Surely there was more to learn? What if we crashed the thing?

By now, the situation in the galley was critical – the kids were hungry, and we were past dinner time. It was also starting to get dark. Gil took over driving while I sprinted between teary kids, cooking dinner in an unfamiliar kitchen (easy meal – pizza and salad) and helping Gil on deck

🪝 One of my favourite parts of this adventure was prepping food and eating together. We were constantly surrounded by beautiful waterways, nature and wildlife

as he steered us into the first mooring spot he could find. We double/triple-checked we'd tied the boat tight enough. I'd imagined cosying up on the first night, enjoying some of the complimentary port and chocolate left out for our arrival, but that didn't happen. We fed the gang and got them clean (enough) and ready for bed. The older two shared the bed at the back, with us in the middle and Rivi in the bed closest to the

galley so we could hear her in the evening if she woke. I realise a bed guard would have been helpful, but instead, we fashioned a bumper using pillows and rolled-up towels. She was happy enough in her snug. Not long after, I was ready to hit the sack myself. The last few hours had been pretty full on, and I was questioning if bringing three children to a confined space on the water was such a great idea...

»→ The slow speed of the canal boat makes it ideal for letting children have a go at steering (or in Rivi's case, just hanging off the tiller)

⬆ The children loved jumping off the boat to walk or run along the canal paths, stretching their legs

REMINDING OURSELVES
– IT'S ENOUGH!

The ocean, diving and marine life are passions that Gil and I share. While Rivi is far too young to be introduced to diving (you've got to be at least ten years old), it's important for us that she grows up knowing water. While a pool is great for confidence and swimming skills, it doesn't compare to natural water. In these spaces, be it a lake, a river or the beach, I'm often at my happiest and can feel an instant connection to nature.

Despite our love of the water and the fact that we are both Divemasters and hold sailing qualifications, being on the water with children made us nervous. We don't do regular paddling sports, so had put canoeing, kayaking or SUPing out of the equation for now, which is how we settled on a canal boat adventure.

There are over 3,380km (2,100 miles) of canal networks in the UK (rivers are the work of nature while canals are artificial, built to carry goods by boat), now mainly used for pleasure and recreation. Other than fleeting memories of watching *Rosie and Jim*, I knew very little about canal boating, so I was surprised to find many hire boat companies available. Most of them allowed children to join and actively promoted their trips as the perfect family adventure.

In terms of safety, it seemed ideal. The boat was steady and slow, and the water still and calm. Except for locks, of course – devices used to help raise or lower boats. Getting through a lock can take 10 to 20 minutes, more if there's a queue, and some stretches on canals had hundreds of them to navigate. But not on the Monmouthshire & Brecon Canal, where we would be cruising. We were instantly attracted to the fact that there were very few locks.

Our initial plan had been to take a route that required us to go through five locks (any way you take is there and back, so that would have been ten locks in total over the trip); there are only a few places along the canal where you can turn the boat, so once you've committed to a route, there is no choice but to get through them all. On the first day, though, I asked Gil if we could re-think our plan to do any locks. I could see he was disappointed, and I was a bit as well, but he agreed with my logic. It takes a minimum of two people to manoeuvre the boat through the locks. The older kids might have been OK to get involved with the task but doing it with a toddler was going to be stressful.

So plan B it was. A medium-paced no-lock route there and back. That plan lasted until the first evening when we swiftly dropped to plan C … let's do the shortest route possible. When adventuring with kids, there's no greater lesson than realising less is more!

⚲ Dulcie and Cooper holding the vessel steady while we moored the boat

LIFE ON BOARD

I was pleased when I woke up on day one feeling considerably more relaxed than the night before. It had been a restful night's sleep; to our surprise, all three children had slept without disruption. I enjoyed the snug feeling of being in our cosy bed, knowing we were on the water tucked in by the quiet and dark canal side.

I was at the tiller on day one. Doing the shortest route, we had about five hours of driving a day, allowing time to moor over lunch and give us all a break and for Gil and me actually to see each other. With just two adults on board, it meant we were always switched on. One would be driving the boat and the other would be tending to the children and sorting meals. My captain experience lasted about an hour before I called for Gil and asked if he wanted to take over. Steering was not my forte. I'd already bumped the sides twice (our driving instructor told us that hitting the side was OK but other boats was not), and each time a canal boat appeared heading our way, my stress levels would rise as I pictured myself causing a crash and sinking us both. Thankfully, Gil enjoyed the task much more than I did and was able to work out how to keep the boat straight. That suited me just fine; I was happy to potter about in the kitchen and with the kids.

It didn't take long to slot into a routine on the canal. We'd set off early while I made breakfast for everyone. After tidying up, the children were free to play with their toys. They'd each brought a bag of toys and

crafts. We'd then get them all outside (lifejackets on), either helping Gil with steering or just walking on the canal side, keeping up with the boat. Dulcie was tasked with reporting the number on each bridge we passed and then working out where we were on the map. Cooper was a self-appointed fisherman. He spent many an hour sitting at the front of the boat with his long stick 'fishing'.

'I caught a fish, I caught a fish!' he yelled with so much excitement one afternoon that I was worried he'd topple over and fall in. He'd come across a dead floating fish. Dragging that poor fish along in the water provided him and his sister with another hour of entertainment (I refused to let him bring it into the boat, to their great disappointment).

Each day, we'd have to fill up our water tank at one of the water points. This was a chance for everyone to have a proper run-around, and I'd keep the children busy by playing 10 Seconds (see page 313). And I'd succumb to

↑ Having a cosy story before bedtime

≫→ When tasks required two adults, we used the sling so we didn't have to worry about Rivi

←≪ With a fully-fitted kitchen, meals are easy to prepare on the canal boat

putting on a film each afternoon for an hour. I hated using screens when escaping them was one of the biggest reasons we went on adventures, but preparing dinner and mooring the boat with grouchy children was enough to tip even the most patient of carers over the edge.

I loved the pace of life on the boat. Pootling along in a tunnel of nature, there was always wildlife to spot and friendly dog walkers to chat with as they passed by. On day one, we were all dressed by mid-morning. We didn't even bother getting out of our pyjamas by the last day. We'd throw our coats and wellies over the top when going outside. When the children went to bed (surprisingly tired at the end of each day despite the slow pace), Gil and I would cosy up in the salon with a drink, fantasising about living on a boat one day.

Our break on *Falcon* had been an excellent little family adventure. A lazy, relaxing break suitable for all ages. We said our goodbyes to *Falcon* and piled into the cars with bruised heads (Gil was the only one who managed to go the whole time without bumping his head even once); some great family memories and lots of promises to return to canal boating one day.

Top tips for a canal boat holiday

• **When choosing a canal boat holiday** as a family, pay attention to the route options available, especially regarding the number of locks you need to pass. Caen Hill Locks and its 29 back-to-back locks may sound fun on paper, but it would probably be exhausting if you were trying to boat through it with young children!

• **We both felt our adventure** would have been more enjoyable if we'd had another adult or shared the experience with another family. The spare pair of adult hands would have made all the difference with splitting steering, cooking and kid-watching duties, leaving more time for sitting and soaking up the views.

• **If you're taking a toddler or baby,** I'd suggest packing a sling. When mooring, filling up water tanks or helping with complex steering manoeuvres, you can safely throw them on your back and still have your hands free to carry out tasks.

• **Try to engage your children** in boating by giving them tasks. This could be keeping track of navigation and noting the numbers on the bridges you pass, helping with steering, assisting with mooring the boat and tying the ropes or attaching the hose for filling the tank.

• **Set rules from the start.** The most important one is not going on deck without telling an adult and always wearing a life vest when outside. We also laid down rules to help keep the boat organised: shoes and coats had a place, and toys needed to be put away after use. A small space like the boat gets messy very quickly if everyone isn't helping to keep it tidy.

• **Get your children into the habit of waving** to passers-by. It's a friendly game that they all loved that led to many interesting chats with strangers.

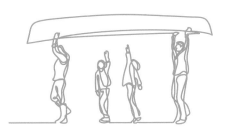

CHILDREN AND

WATER SAFETY

You can't be too vigilant around water, and it's not an environment you want to be taking risks in – especially around inland open water, which statistically is the most dangerous to children. Almost half of those who lose their life to drowning each year never intended to be in the water in the first place, showing that the same level of vigilance is needed for simply being around water as if you are planning to be in the water.

Without a doubt, fitting your children with a personal flotation device (PFD) is the single most important thing you can do before participating in any water activity. Adults should also be wearing PFDs if doing paddle sports. Fitting your children with a PFD will ensure that they are pushed safely to the surface if they fall in. The straps must be secure and snug for the PFD to work effectively.

When getting a PFD for a child, check that it:

- is the right PFD for your child's weight and age
- has a strap that goes between their legs
- has a large collar to support their head in the water
- has a grab handle behind the neck.

We've found that the best PFD on the market for young children is the Peak UK Kidz Zip. It provides all the safety of a life jacket (including having the head support that will right them in the water with their head up) while providing the comfort of a buoyancy aid (which are less bulky than a life jacket but usually come without the head support). They are bright, easy to fit and come in two sizes: Sproglet for two to four year olds and Sprog for four to seven year olds.

We've also found that having a wetsuit and a UV suit has been helpful for days spent by rivers and on the beach and for protecting

children from the elements. The wetsuit allows children to spend longer playing in the water without getting cold. The UV suit is great for protecting them from the sun on hot days (make sure it's UV protected and ideally long-sleeved for ultimate protection).

Sun reflecting on the water increases the risk of sunburn, so always put lots of sunscreen on your children if you're on or near water, even on a cloudy day.

←« »→ The Peak UK Kidz Zip is a great PDF to keep infants and small children safe near water

SEVEN ESSENTIAL RULES
AROUND WATER

1 TEACH YOUR CHILDREN TO SWIM

All family members must know how to swim confidently if you intend to be in or around water. Make sure everyone can do these five water survival safety skills:

1 jump into water over their head and return to the surface
2 turn around in the water and orient to safety
3 tread water and/or float
4 combine breathing with forward movement in the water
5 exit the water

2 WEAR YOUR PFD AT ALL TIMES

Children should be wearing their PFD at all times when they're in or on the water. Make sure they are fitted correctly.

3 PICK A BEACH WITH LIFEGUARDS

Throughout peak seasons, many UK beaches are patrolled by lifeguards. While you still need to remain vigilant of your children, the lifeguards will display (using flags) where it is safe to be in the water, monitor the currents and weather, and be on hand for a rescue if needed.

Use the RNLI website to search lifeguarded beaches. It will show you on what dates they'll be there and at what times: www.rnli.org/find-my-nearest

4 BE WELL-INFORMED

Before taking part in any water adventure, you should be well-informed of anything that might impact your journey. This includes weather forecasts, tide times (especially knowing when high tide is on a beach) and checking any danger warnings surrounding weirs.

5 CONSTANTLY RISK ASSESS

When you're with children in, on or near water, you need to constantly assess the situation for danger. Look for changes in weather or currents, any potentially dangerous boats or debris approaching, and your children behaving sensibly. You should have your children in sight at all times.

6 TEACH YOUR CHILDREN WATER SAFETY

Before getting anywhere near water, you should explain what is and isn't safe to do when around or in water. Children should be told what to do if they get into trouble (wave their arms above their heads and call for help) and how to call for help if they spot someone else in trouble.

Teach children that if they get caught in a rip current, swimming towards the beach is ineffective as you'll be swimming against the current. Instead, they should swim parallel to the shore until the rip current spits them out.

Weirs are another danger as you can get caught in a circulating stopper (a whirlpool). If this happens, you can try to swim down or sideways to exit the circuit. Higher river flow increases the chances and strength of a stopper.

7 BE CAUTIOUS WITH INFLATABLES

Inflatables – such as rubber rings or blow-up boats – are good fun but can easily be dragged away in currents or winds. If using inflatables, instruct children to stay close to shore.

SOUTH COAST SAILING EXPEDITION

by Tobina Marx

BEING ON THE WATER brings adventure, calm, escape from busy lives, togetherness, learning and laughs. It's why we love sailing so much as a family.

Francis, Bodie's father, has spent years on board various sailing boats, working his way up from deck scrubber to skipper. He has taken part in many voyages, including the Fastnet Race, which can be full of high winds, fast boats and challenging sailing (although ironically, the year he did it, there was barely a lick of wind, so it was more a case of whether the boat would crawl back home in time for us to catch the plane for our first holiday together!). I've also spent large amounts of time on the water myself, spending bygone summers on the lakes of Canada, learning the ins and outs of boats of every shape, from canoes to small tippy sailing boats.

When we had our son, Bodie, the year after getting married, we loved the idea of introducing him early to sailing life. So, at 14 weeks old, we set off on our first sojourn on our boat (which we share with three other families), taking all the kit on the wheelbarrow down the pontoon to the little dory boat, which we used to take us out to the sailing boat.

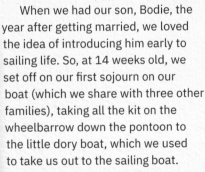

In the early days, the boat functioned like a floating camper van. We learned and honed the logistics and new strategies to amuse, make safe and enjoy having a six-month-old, a nine-month-old and then a crawling, toddling little person on board. To add to the mayhem, we even added a puppy who had to be trained and introduced slowly to boat life, too. Our kit became a little sleeker with each trip, and we also enjoyed introducing other families with kids to the adventures. Those trips were the highlight of our summers!

THE SOUTH COAST, AS A NEW ADVENTURE TEAM

Life is never a straight line, and our journey evolved, too, with an unexpected twist. We separated in 2021, but with the determination and grace to be a loving co-parenting family in a new set-up. The boat became one of the places where we could set out to sea as just us wherever we were and let the adventures take precedence.

Last summer, when our son was four, we mapped out an expedition along the south coast with the three of us as the constant team with various cousins, dogs and friends either jumping on board for a night or two, or meeting up with families on other boats that would raft up alongside or drop anchor nearby.

The seas heading west can be choppy at certain points, so Francis set off on a 36-hour mission with two other dads to have the boat drop anchor at Worbarrow Bay. The first challenge was here – the car park is a good 20-minute walk from the bay, so some pretty decent kit preparation was required and strong carrying muscles were tested. Planning a week's worth of meals and snacks is no mean feat with a small fridge on board and limited cupboard

stowing places. It is indeed a fine art, but regardless, we were still fairly heavily laden!

The joy of this remote bay is that it feels like a place of magic in the evenings as the beach-going day crowds head off before the car park barrier shuts and the sun slowly drops on those left behind aboard various boats.

We then set off east, back along the coast, hugging the various cliffs and bays, adjusting to our new pace of hoisting sails, enjoying long stretches of passages on board and then dropping anchor in various places to explore, stretch the legs and play in the water.

The first day also brought the realisation that bringing two water guns was a game-changer in getting our boy out on the paddleboard and into the sea swimming because as long as it meant spraying Mama endlessly, then he was game for anything!

One of the greatest joys at sea as a family is just the time spent tinkering, sometimes with barely any chat and sometimes lots of laughs and unexpected events. The chilled moments range from doing Lego projects on deck or down below in the cosy cabin to reading the odd book when possible as the sails blow the boat along (more so these days now that Bodie can walk about more safely on his own), to staring out to sea at the ever-changing landscapes while on the wheel or taking the best spot in the house – the bow (front) of the boat. Then, moments later, a shriek when Francis's phone drops overboard (again!), a pigeon flies into the cabin, or a critical piece of Lego rolls dangerously near a hole that could drop out to the sea. It's ever unpredictable and ever entertaining.

We have been lucky and only had two passages of more choppy waters where the boys (by this point, our nephew, who is the same age as Bodie and an excellent crew team member, had joined us) felt a little green, and one of them

was sick. This required a whole new level of multitasking for this mama, holding on as the boat lurched over the waves while trying to clear up the cabin with a bucket and rags! On these passages, the boys tended to become very sleepy thanks to the rocking motion and snuggled into one of our laps for a snooze. Then as soon as the seas settled and we arrived at our next anchor point, they would wake up like a jack-in-the-box, ready to help on board and get exploring on nearby shores.

Depending on how close to shore we are, we will either jump on to paddleboards and explore the bay, take the tender into the beach for a sand castle mission or ice cream, or hit the coast path for a good walk. Lunch and tea range from setting up a picnic and barbecue on the beach if allowed, cooking on board with the small but perfectly functional oven or gas top, or finding a walkable pub or cafe for a treat outing.

SOUTH COAST SAILING EXPEDITION

One of our favourite spots from the trip was around Brownsea Island, where we played on paddleboards in the wide, gentle shallows mid-morning and popped into Tesco in bare feet and lifejackets on the beach at Poole. Two hours later, we were exploring the island with barely a soul around while the boat sat calmly tucked into a shallow bay off the National Trust-owned island.

HEARTS FULL OF ADVENTURE

Of course, with the magic come misdemeanours, breakdowns and mishaps, such as the boat getting stuck in the mud and needing to wait five hours to get off when the tide came back up. Yes, there is a lot of packing, unpacking and boat faff and frustrating things that go wrong at sea. And there is always the wonderfully unpredictable weather of the UK to plan around. But these challenges are all part of the team spirit-building process, and there is nothing like reflecting on a day of adventures over a glass of wine as the children snore in their cabins.

The kids are learning about adventures, challenges, new skills, water confidence, making new friends and cementing old ones, letting go of routines

and house rules and finding a new balance on board a 6 x 2.5m (20 x 8ft) container that rocks from side to side. In time and as Bodie grows, so will the type of sailing adventures we go on. Hopefully, he will take up the helm on the wheel with glee, and as the teenage years loom, we will no doubt see him hopping off on his own to see friends on boats next door or meet on the beach. We will see if his enthusiasm for the boat, which is currently very strong, continues each year and what it brings us as a family.

The last afternoon is often melancholy for me as we head back to reality, hair windswept and probably all needing a good bath, with bags

full of slightly damp clothes and sandy spades but hearts full of adventure and memories. It is the combination of both time slowing down, days merging and losing their relevance, and the quiet spots of just being that make time at sea so special – it is why my greatest hope is that we will be spending time at sea with loved ones for many years to come.

PADDLING

ADVENTURES

Paddling sports are a good fit for families as they can be gentle, allow you to carry weight (children and gear) easily, and are adaptable. When babies are old enough to sit and wear a PFD, you can start taking children with you paddling. Children can begin learning to paddle from the age of five, but it's only around age eight that they are likely to be competent enough to go solo.

If you're paddling with young children or starting out with older children stick to calm and easy waters. This means on rivers, sticking to grade one routes suitable for beginners (rivers are graded from one to six, one being easiest and six being very challenging). If at sea, stick to shorelines and only when the sea is calm. As well as following water safety guidelines

(see page 236) and wearing a PFD, you should also pack with you a throw-line if you're participating in any paddling sports.

The best way to get children engaged with paddling sports is to start them young. Mix up paddling with lots of breaks and time splashing and playing in the water. And always look out for the three biggest beginner mistakes: holding the paddle the wrong way, looking at your feet rather than ahead and paddling downwind.

CANOEING AND KAYAKING

↑ Canoe or kayak?

Canoeing is perhaps the easiest paddling activity to do as a family. Canoes are big and stable, giving you lots of space to fit in adults and children and gear if you want to do a longer trip. For a family of four (two adults, two children), look for a canoe that is 4.9–5.5m (16–18ft) long. When the children are old enough to paddle confidently and steer by themselves (usually around the age of eight), you'll need two canoes or might want to move to using kayaks. Even before your children can paddle, it's a good idea to bring a spare paddle with you so they can practise. There are child-size paddles suitable for different ages.

When canoeing, comfortable seats and backrests for all the family will make for a more enjoyable trip. You also need to think about napping if your child still needs them. You need to provide them with an insulating base (the bottom of the canoe is as cold as the water) and something to throw over the canoe (like a waterproof or small tarp) to shade them.

The adult in the stern (back) of the boat is the person who is steering and needs full attention, so distracting toddlers and babies are best placed with the adult in the front of the boat.

Kayaks are easier to manoeuvre and faster but also less stable. A child as young as four could join an adult in a double kayak, with the adult at the back. A child of this age isn't going to provide much propulsion, so your distances will be limited. From eight years old, children can start to improve their paddling and stamina skills and might be ready to start

↑ You can start introducing children to kayaking independently from around age eight

going out in a solo kayak. When starting to kayak by themselves, get your child to practise turning, accelerating and stopping. They will also need to learn how to capsize and get back in their boat from the water. This is an important skill to learn and one that might scare children, so it's probably best for them to learn it with an experienced instructor if you are not competent to teach it yourself.

For both kayaking and canoeing, expect to get a bit wet from splashing paddles and for there to be some water on the floor. Children should be wearing quick-dry fabrics with sandals in warm weather and booties and waterproofs in colder weather. Pack plenty of spare dry and warm clothes protected in a waterproof bag.

STAND UP PADDLEBOARDING (SUPING)

SUPing is a fun and easy sport to pick up but children should only SUP if they are confident swimmers. Make sure they have all the correct gear before setting off and ensure they wear the appropriate board leash at all times.

Small children (under five) will need to be with an adult – sitting, kneeling or standing on the bow of the board. This is a good way for them to start getting a feel for balancing and manoeuvring. From age five, your child might be ready to start SUPing by themselves. Many find it easier to start kneeling down, moving to standing once they've built up their confidence. Get them to practise turning left and right, accelerating and decelerating, falling and jumping off the board and getting back on the board from the water.

Children can use adult SUPs but might find it easier to learn and manoeuvre if they have a child-specific board. Boards have different buoyancies which are measured in volumes. As a general rule for beginners, get a buoyancy that is double the user's weight; so if your child is 40kg (6st 5lb), you'll want a volume of at least 80 litres. As you build your technique and get better at paddling, you'll need less volume so, hopefully, the child will grow with the board.

On colder days, wearing a wetsuit and booties will help keep your children warm. On a hot day, a UV suit will protect them from the sun and they can paddle barefoot (although booties might still be a good idea if entry to and from the water might be rocky).

You can start introducing children to SUP independently from around age five

THE UK'S BEST PADDLING ADVENTURES

Once you're competent in a canoe or kayak, you might be ready to take on a bigger multi-day adventure as a family. Meandering down rivers in the day and enjoying riverside campsites or accommodation at night is a perfect combination!

We have some great runs in the UK, all providing good views and interesting wildlife-spotting opportunities. Most also have a range of hire companies that can transport you, your canoe/kayak and gear from the start and end of your trip.

RIVER WYE, ENGLAND (133KM/83 MILES)

The River Wye is an idyllic river and perhaps the most popular for paddle adventures. Most people do the full route in a week, although you can take a much more leisurely pace if you prefer. In good weather, the river is safe to navigate. With plenty of pubs, cafes, hotels and campsites on the riverfront, organising a family adventure here is easy.

GREAT GLEN CANOE TRAIL, SCOTLAND (96KM/60 MILES)

This route combines natural lochs and man-made waterways on the Caledonian Canal. This is a popular multi-day canoe trip meaning there are lots of hire companies and campsites en route to making planning a breeze. You'll need to be ready to portage across the 29 lochs. Paddlers should be experienced with open water paddling or team up with a group or instructor.

RIVER SPEY, SCOTLAND (172KM/107 MILES)

The Spey is one of the longest rivers in the UK, located on the edge of the Cairngorms National Park. The river is a mix of flat water and lochs, gently moving water and grade two rapids (sometimes grade three, depending on the weather). Look out for ospreys, otters and the salmon population that swims in the waters. Several whisky production facilities sit on the water's edge.

RIVER THAMES, ENGLAND; FROM OXFORD TO WINDSOR (105KM/65 MILES)

Cover a stretch of the UK's most famous river, the Thames. The three-day Oxford to Windsor challenge (it can be spread over four days if you want to go slower) is littered with well-maintained campsites and plenty of pubs. The waters are calm and you'll be sharing the river with rowers and day-boaters.

THE HEBRIDES, SCOTLAND

If you are looking for something
a bit more adventurous, then
head to the Hebrides. Marine
life and beautiful coastlines are
abundant in Muck, Eigg, Rum and
Canna, the group of islands west
of Arisaig known as 'the Small
Isles'. Explore the islands at your
own pace, finding idyllic spots
to camp (wild camping is legal).
This is an adventure only suitable
for experienced paddlers who
are confident taking on this sea
kayaking expedition. You'll need to
be self-sufficient and comfortable
doing big open water crossings.

RIVER TWEED, ENGLAND AND SCOTLAND
(110KM/68 MILES)

The Tweed is a quiet, lesser-
known river that can be run from
Peebles to Berwick-upon-Tweed,
providing 110km (68 miles) of
uninterrupted paddling. This
usually takes three to four days
to cover. En route, you'll pass by
historic buildings, grand castles
and also run close to Hadrian's
Wall, making it a great option
for history enthusiasts.

Calm paddling and epic views

KAYAKING THE GREAT GLEN CANOE TRAIL

by Simon Margot

WE RAISED OUR GIRLS on camping holidays, river swimming and hill walking so they've always been adventurous. I recall the girls and their mum laughing aloud in driving sleet as we descended a hill walk on a wintry holiday. I felt happy that we'd raised resilient little people.

Lily, our oldest, has always been wild. Annabelle, her little sister, prefers to know what to expect and to follow a plan, as does Mary, their mum. Our family adventures are therefore tailored to suit the group: either we stick together and follow a plan, or sometimes Lily and I will be the trailblazers and Annabelle and Mary will join us another time.

Our first kayak camp was along a local section of calm river we are very familiar with, to a campsite on the river we knew to have good facilities. It was October, but the weather was good. Lily was nine, and we were confident she could comfortably paddle the 9.7km (6 miles). We had all day and plenty of

places to rest and picnic along the way. We took a tent and an electric heater in the kayak, which was amazing. We paddled back the next day with big grins from the sense of adventure and achievement. Over many similar trips, we gradually refined our kit choices, and Annabelle soon joined us, with Mary meeting us in the car as she doesn't enjoy paddling.

When nurturing the girls' sense of adventure in various settings, I try not to overstep the mark and either put them in danger or a miserable situation where they have a negative experience. Ideally, I help them learn the fine line between adventure and disaster, risk and harm.

PREPARATION

Lily first mentioned the Great Glen Canoe Trail (GGCT) after her Scout leader had told her about it, knowing that we'd done a few kayak camping trips. Some research online and tips from the Scout leader convinced me it was achievable for Lily and me. The route is 97km (60 miles), which we could comfortably manage if we allowed four or five days. Lily was still keen after knowing more about it; this was key, as if she was going to enjoy the challenge, she needed to be invested.

In preparation for the trip, we planned a challenging weekend paddle of Lake Windermere. We did this in winter, so I booked the YHA Ambleside Hostel on the north end of the lake and left the car at the south end overnight, in the National Trust Fell Foot car park.

The conditions were rough, so it was challenging but a great experience of a long paddle (19km/12 miles each way) in a large body of water, testing our kit, food and drinking arrangements, and landing on awkward banks to rest. We had a great night in the hostel and enjoyed the paddle back to the car in better

conditions the next day. That night, I returned to our table from ordering dinner at the hostel to find Lily researching walking routes and weather forecasts for the next day; she picked a great route to climb to finish off our trip.

As a result of this trip, we both knew our sea/touring kayaks were well suited to paddling long distances, and we had windproof, waterproof clothes and layers we could use as conditions dictated. Lily used a large water bladder in her bag with a flexible drinking straw for all-day hydration and we learned good refuelling strategies consisting of cereal bars, nuts, fruit and sweets. Although sweets are a great source of morale and calories for Lily on long journeys, she agreed to a limit of one bag a day.

PLANNING

The trail goes from the west coast of Scotland near Fort William and Ben Nevis, north-east to Inverness on the east coast. The water is mostly flat, except along Loch Ness – a large, exposed body of water that can get choppy. The scenery along the route is stunning and peaceful; it's an epic journey of a lifetime.

I did a LOT of research online; the area I'm not familiar with is further than we'd kayaked before, so I wanted to be prepared for as many eventualities as possible. I had to first check for insurmountable dangers or obstacles, such as water features beyond our skill or fitness. I found lots of reliable information online as the trail is well supported by the authorities and well-trodden.

I chose to make the trip in summer for long daylight hours and less chance of inclement weather. In Scotland, this means midges, so we planned the trip for early summer and packed lots of midge repellent. Summer outdoors always requires careful sun protection, so we both chose wide-brimmed hats and long-sleeved tops we were comfortable paddling in all day. There are long portages on the route, so we took a fold-up trolley to move the kayaks, as they're heavy when full of camping gear and food.

I always take a tow rope so I can attach to Lily's kayak if she needs assistance or a rest (I have a quick-release system in case the rope gets tangled). Another handy item for Lily was a neoprene swim hat for rough conditions. It keeps her head warm and dry, her hair out of her eyes and won't blow off.

A big headache for the GGCT was getting the kayaks back from the end after leaving the car at the start. We could get the train back from the end, and then drive the car to pick up the kayaks, but this would be a tiresome end to the trip and poor preparation for the long drive home. After much pondering, I found a car moving company and arranged for them to move my car from the start to the end of the trail, and I carried the spare key. This worked very well, for not much more than we would have spent on train tickets. I could leave booking the car transport and confirming the pick-up point until the week before we left so I could check the weather forecast and paddle in the direction of the most favourable wind.

We took a small camping stove and instant dehydrated food as its light to carry, and we knew we had access to water for cooking all along the route. The route is straightforward to navigate, but I printed a map well in advance, which I sealed in waterproof sheets with camping/ rest sites marked; this allowed us to track our progress and decide where to rest.

Because we weren't sure how far we would paddle each day, we didn't make a firm plan of where to camp, as there are plenty of options, and we could wild camp as a last resort. If we didn't cover the whole distance in time, or if we had an accident or injury that prevented us from completing the trail, I planned to leave the kayaks and get a taxi to the car at the end of the trail and collect the kayaks later. I always think it's prudent to consider what you will do in various worst-case scenarios, to avoid panic if it happens.

THE TRIP

We started at Banavie for the free car park, and to skip the portage of eight locks called Neptune's Staircase. It took a while on arrival to find the office back in Corpach where we paid £10 for a key to access the toilets and showers at the free campsites along the route. I handed over the car key to the car moving company, and we were soon underway.

The first day, we soaked up the stunning scenery, including Ben Nevis in the backdrop. Lily spent much of the day grinning at the crystal-clear and smooth water, reflecting green hills and blue skies. We covered 24km (15 miles) and camped at Laggan Locks on the north end of Loch Lochy – this was one of the most stunning campsites I'd ever experienced.

The next day, we set off refreshed and soon reached the only significant resupply point on the route, Fort Augustus, a pretty village right on the canal with lots of shops. We were well stocked, so we didn't need any shopping but we took the chance to stop for a proper meal. We were to be grateful for that meal, as Fort Augustus is the gateway to Loch Ness, the most challenging part of the route.

A headwind soon picked up, making the going slow and conditions choppy. We started on the west bank and should have switched to the east for shelter from the wind and better camping options, but hindsight is a wonderful thing and crossing the large expanse was daunting, so we kept hugging the shore. As conditions were difficult, we decided to camp at the first opportunity. The trail follows the west bank, and the map showed a campsite at Alltsigh, but this wasn't visible when we got there, and with no obvious landing we continued through the afternoon and evening into the headwind till we reached Urquhart Castle. We went to bed exhausted without even cooking tea.

Waking up to the castle in daylight with the outlook on to Loch Ness was impressive and gave us some enthusiasm for the day ahead. It was when reviewing the map we realised we had covered 40km (25 miles) the previous day and were over halfway along the trail. After a quick breakfast to beat the arrival of castle visitors, we were underway to brave the second half of Loch

Ness. Because we had plenty of time and supplies, we took a more leisurely pace and included some stops on beautiful sheltered gravel beaches and reached the north end after lunchtime. We were within striking distance of the end of the trail. We could have camped at this point and had an easy couple of days, but Lily was keen to crack on to a takeaway at the end and get on the way home. The final stretch to Inverness was calm, sheltered and sunny and felt like a victory lap after the passage of Loch Ness.

On arrival at Inverness, we quickly found the car and got the kayaks loaded, then got Lily her well-earned nuggets and milkshake before we started the long drive home overnight.

REFLECTIONS

Even at the time, Lily and I could feel this had been a special experience, and so it has proved in our history. There's nothing I would change in hindsight, as things could easily have gone worse if we'd made other choices and the things that went wrong, we learned from. The trip wasn't just about the journey. It was about us getting to the point where we were both capable of doing it and felt comfortable doing it together. And since this trip, Lily has continued adventuring, kayaking to the Isle of Wight through the Needles to go paragliding at age 12.

I look forward to the day when Annabelle nudges me in the ribs and asks when we're going on an adventure!

SURFING

Surfing is fun for all the family and a good way to enjoy the outdoors on a summer's day by the beach. From around age seven, most children are ready to start learning. Before this, you may be able to start them on bodyboards or surfing with an adult, helping them to catch a wave and balance. Lessons will help them learn the best technique for balancing and catching a wave.

Before heading out surfing, make sure you carry out a risk assessment on the beach you intend to head to and the weather; it's a good idea to use beaches with lifeguards.

Surfing is the only watersport for which your child won't wear a PFD as it's too bulky and will prevent them from being able to surf properly,

Children can start learning to surf from around seven years, but before that they can play and splash about on bodyboards

so you'll need to be extra vigilant. You also need to make sure that your children are looking around them before catching any wave, making

sure they aren't too close to other surfers, which could cause a collision in the water. They should wear their safety leash at all times in the water.

Pre-teen children will require a small, soft board (known as a foamy). These soft boards reduce the risk of injury and are light and easy for them to carry. Most surf beaches have places where you can hire surfboards, which may be a good alternative to buying and transporting your own board.

←« A few surf lessons early on will help teach your children the right technique for surfing

»→ Cliff Beach, Isle of Lewis

BEST FAMILY-FRIENDLY SURF SPOTS IN THE UK

CORNWALL, ENGLAND

Cornwall has lots of family-friendly surfing beaches, including Newquay and Watergate Bay.

GOWER PENINSULA, WALES

Langland, Caswell, Rhossili and Llangennith are all beaches offering great surf and lessons.

ISLE OF LEWIS, SCOTLAND

A beautiful island with consistent waves for all levels.

NORTH YORKSHIRE, ENGLAND

Cayton Bay, Whitby, Saltburn-by-the-Sea and Bridlington offer some of the best beginner surfing spots in the area.

DEVON, ENGLAND

Westward Ho! is a firm favourite for beginners. For more challenging waves, Croyde Bay is considered one of the best spots for surfing in the UK.

GUERNSEY, CHANNEL ISLANDS

Vazon Bay has shallow waters, perfect for surfing with young kids.

COUNTY CORK, NORTHERN IRELAND

There are lots of stunning surf beaches to choose from but Inchydoney is ideal for families.

BRISTOL, ENGLAND

The Wave in Bristol is an artificial surf spot providing more than 1,000 waves every hour, ranging from beginner to expert level.

PEMBROKESHIRE, WALES

With 3km (1.8 miles) of sandy beach, Newgale is one of the best family-friendly spots for surfing in Pembrokeshire.

ADVENTURE PARC SNOWDONIA, WALES

The UK's first inland surf lagoon, delivering waves to suit all levels.

The best surfer in the line-up is the one with the biggest smile

SURFING

by Gareth Davies

@creakyslider

SHORTLY AFTER YET MORE SURGERY to repair my rugby-broken skeleton, Seren decided, at four years old, that she wanted to have a go at this thing her big brother was doing. Very soon I found myself in the water pushing her on big foamies into waves; big brother had slowly fallen out of love with surfing, so it was just Seren and me. She paddled everywhere, springing up on to her soft-top as I lumbered about with my six fused vertebrae on my longboard.

We'd only been at it a few months and were on an even playing field even with the 39 years between us. Together, we were learning to paddle, to balance, to pop up, sitting at the top at Sennen Cove looking down to the sea, trying to read the surf, read a wave before getting wet. Having something to do that we were both learning from scratch certainly added a new dynamic to our relationship. There was the physical challenge, but also the mental stimulation, her little voice encouraging me and giving me tips, pointing things out to me in

the water. Most importantly, the smiles, the 'stoked' chats about this wave or that over our Blue Lagoon hot chocolate special and battered sausage – the post-surf snack of champions – while we debriefed our novice journey as peers (in the same way that I'd offer advice to her as a father in many other parts of our lives). There were laughs, frustrations and lots of smiling.

BIG LUMP OF HAPPINESS IN MY THROAT

That first full year we surfed a lot, as much as we could, every day when we were back in Cornwall, sometimes twice a day ... then it was weekends only when school started, and half-term meant plunging into the cooling autumnal water. Then I saw the grit of my little lady as winter rolled in; she still wanted to be in the water, so the challenge was laid down, and how could I say no? Me at 1.96m (6ft 5in), Shrek, the ex-professional rugby player and my tiny, feral, little lady ... so in we went. Fewer people in the water, more swell, more waves and more time for learning. Lessons for Seren embedding the foundations of surf technique, etiquette and safety during which she got bored of Dad's voice...

watching her soak it all up, rubbing shoulders with former and future pro surfers and British Champions. Then regurgitating it when she was asked to deliver the safety message to other students in her lessons. I was so very impressed. It was just one of the little things I've seen her do that has shown me her incredible resilience and ability to meet challenges head-on. Definitely a smart move by Dad.

That Christmas saw us venture away from the waves in West Penwith on our first overseas surf trip – Baleal Island in Portugal beckoned. A lovely and quiet little spot close to Peniche, with good winter swell, threw up another challenge for both of us ... bigger regular waves, which Seren attacked without hesitation, putting her trust in Dad and her new surf coaches. Showing no fear and always laughing and smiling, she showed me the way. We were walking to the beach in Baleal early one morning when Seren said something that told me how much she loved this new activity we'd taken on: 'Daddy, when I am surfing, I get a big lump of happiness in my throat'.

TAKING SURFING FURTHER

After another trip to Portugal and one to Lanzarote early the following year, the lockdowns restricted our water time. Living in a landlocked county it was then on to dry land training, and again this was taken on with such enthusiasm,

Seren pushing me to get my arse into gear. Training in the garden using balance boards and doing press-ups, all incorporated into home-school timetables. As soon as amendments to rules were made for single parents and bubbles, we were away back to the family in Cornwall, where we managed to juggle my job, Seren's home-schooling and slotting surfing into the curriculum as PE. We were in the water at sunrise, then again at sunset – immersed in it for four solid months, and it was just wonderful. We regained a lost connection with nature, learned respect for Mother Nature and the power of the sea – and

read what Neptune was throwing at us to play with ... how to dance best with his waves. Geography lessons included more marine and coast content; sub-sea topography, offshore weather, currents, marine life – learning for both dad and daughter.

We continued to progress and enjoy ourselves. There'd be simple chatter as we'd get us and the boards ready and walk down the hill to our local spot and paddle out together, sharing and laughing. All of a sudden, in the right conditions, we were surfing together, choosing where to go, watching and reading the break before going in. Our first 'party wave' (catching a wave together) was something neither of us will forget. It happened in the middle of winter when we were alone in the line-up messing about and trying to keep warm – then paddling, laughing and gliding into the shore a few metres apart; it was a shared moment that will stay with us for ever.

We were hooked, but schools were open again and lives were supposed to get back to some sort of normality. Ours wouldn't – we'd experienced too much and our trajectories had veered too far to return to how things had been. The idea of moving to the south-west tip of our island was firmly embedded. Surfing had pushed all Seren's other sports and hobbies to one side, and she was single-minded and focussed.

BONNIE AND BIGGER WAVES

This is where we met Bonnie, who's changed our lives. Bonnie is our old Ford Transit converted camper. Nowadays, she's ready to go at the end of every week. Friday afternoon now means the school collection is done in the camper, and we're off – having watched reports and spoken to friends through the week, we decide where we're going as we hit the road. My co-pilot/navigator/DJ ensures that wherever we go, we have a clear road, a full tummy and good tunes in our ears. Those long drives are another fantastic thing that have come from our surfing. The conversations we have while we clock up the mileage are so open and in-depth – nothing is off the table, and what I've learned as a dad and what it's done for our relationship is just so important. We now have a young lady in the house who will come and talk to me about anything. This has further embedded an already close relationship, but the trust builds between us in the water, along with all of the other activities we manage to squeeze in on our trips: fishing, making fire, cliff jumping, harbour jumping, snorkelling, diving.

We recently went on our first big trip, to Indonesia; Seren was ready, I was ready, so off we went, both of us only ever having surfed in wetsuits before and on sandy shores or banks. Now we were in boardies (boardshorts), over shallow volcanic reefs and powerful surf in warm water. How would she tackle this? There was no hesitation. I followed as she paddled out some 800m (875 yards) into the line-up over the reef and proceeded to clean up, wave after wave, laughing and giggling, even managing a high five as she cruised past me when I paddled back out. Watching her doing her thing from afar – confident, polite and happy – was truly a proud dad moment.

For those parents thinking about whether their kids should give it a go – don't think twice. Let your kids feel the incredible and unique feeling of going into one of Mother Nature's playgrounds and sliding along a wave. How to do it? We are lucky to have surf schools all around the country now, and my advice would be to use them – they are the experts, and it's not just about getting you on to your board and on to a wave, but also how to be safe in the water and to know what to do when in the line-up – not understanding that part is like knowing how to drive a car but never having read the Highway Code.

After that, the world is your oyster – get among it! Listen to the laughter. The phrase we heard early on is now our mantra when in the water: 'The best surfer in the line-up is the one with the biggest smile.' Keep that in mind, and you won't go far wrong.

WILD SWIMMING

If your kids are confident swimmers, then wild (or outdoor) swimming is a great activity to do as a family – from swimming in the sea or spending a hot day splashing in a nearby river to hiking to hidden tarns or waterfalls for a dip.

Second to water safety and fitting children with a PFD (follow the guidelines on page 236), staying warm will be your biggest concern. Outdoor bodies of water are cold, even in summer. The cold will affect children far more than adults, so you need to be prepared for this.

One of the easiest ways to keep them warm is to put them in a well-fitted wetsuit. Take regular breaks out of the water to hydrate, have a snack and check their temperature. If they feel cold (looking pale, blue, shivering or cold on the back of their neck or chest), then take a break from the water. Have a towel and dry clothes available to get them warm quickly. It's a good idea to have a warm fleece to hand (even on a hot day). Ensure they

are hydrated and have eaten some food, ideally something warm like hot chocolate or soup. Get them running around playing a game like tag, to warm them up quickly.

Water shoes are a good idea. They will make it easier for your children to get in and out of the water and will prevent them from slipping or stepping on sharp objects that they may not be able to see.

The water quality in UK rivers or canals can make them unstable for swimming; this tends to be more the case near urban areas or after flooding. If you are concerned about water quality, cover cuts with waterproof plasters, keep your children's faces out of the water and wash your hands with antibacterial gel before eating anything.

←« »→ Wild swimming is a great activity to do with children. Make sure you keep them warm and they wear a PFD until they are confident swimmers

Adapting adventures for children
with additional needs

WILDERNESS SWIMMING AND PLUNGE POOLS

by Charlie Ward

MY LOVE OF THE OUTDOORS properly began when I went on my first outdoor residential camp as a teenager. I had such a brilliant experience during that week, finally finding a place where I thrived, doing activities that matched my skill set. I never found this in the classroom, perhaps because of my late dyslexia diagnosis. From that point on, I decided I wanted to help others experience the benefits of being outdoors, which affects us all positively, both mentally and physically. I'm now a mother to two amazing little people – Tristan, age nine and Lyla, age eight – as well as being a part-time PE teacher and forest school instructor.

During pregnancy, I did not want to take any risks, so I stopped all my adventuring and only went on gentle walks. I even had a crazy moment and sold all my outdoor climbing gear, something that I went on to regret (I'm going to blame that on the baby brain!). Once I'd had my children, I began to realise that this wasn't something I had to give up. My partner and I were determined to find ways to ensure that the outdoors remained a large and important part of family life.

We began introducing our children to outdoor activities from a young age. In time, we built up their skills so they could manage more difficult terrain,

gradients and lengths. We tried to give them as much independence as possible, so they learned how to manage their own equipment and temperature levels. This was key to advancing to more challenging adventures.

As a family, we take part in loads of different activities, but one of our most loved is wilderness swimming and plunge pool jumping. These give us the freedom to explore the outdoors in a fun way: enjoying being in the water on our own terms, not confined to swimming timetables

or busy changing rooms. Along the way to our intended water spot, we always look out for wildlife, learning about flora and fauna. It has all the makings of a perfect family adventure!

NANTCOL WATERFALLS ADVENTURE

One of our favourite wilderness swimming adventures was exploring Nantcol Waterfalls and then wilderness camping in the Rhinogs, Wales. The plan was to take all our wetsuits and camping stuff with us. It was a team effort as we had to share the weight between us to ensure we had all the necessary things to keep warm, dry and happy. The plan was to stop and explore and swim in the streams, plunge pools and lakes along the way to and from the wilderness camp.

The weather was glorious as we headed out on a Friday summer's evening. The adventure started off with a little bit of whinging, which was usual with Tristan due to his additional needs. He gets apprehensive on an adventure, unsure of what to expect. This is just his learning style, and he needs to ask loads of questions to settle his mind and then we are all good to go.

We found a cool place to swim early on, just by a little waterfall with cliff sides we could jump off. After getting wetsuited up and with life jackets on,

I explored the depth of the water to make sure it was safe. Tristan and Lyla had such an amazing time in the water splashing and jumping that we went well over schedule and ended up needing to change our intended camping location. One of the great things about wilderness camping is that you have the flexibility to do this.

Once we had all had enough of the water, it was time to get dry and put our walking boots back on to walk up to our camping spot. Getting changed has to be quite a smooth, quick transition to make sure everyone stays warm. Although getting the wetsuit booties off is always a struggle when they get wet, they are an essential bit of kit to keep everyone's feet nice and safe from stones and any hidden sharp objects such as broken glass.

Once we reached our camping spot, we set up the tent and began sharing our day's adventures while heating up and eating our ration packs. The children had loved the plunge pool so much that they begged to return the same way so they could go back to the same spot. We were happy to let them lead the adventure!

I will always remember this trip and the children's faces when they saw where we were going to swim. It was a beautiful location with rocks, moss and trees surrounding the water and waterfall – a timeless space that resonated with natural beauty and the echoes of every child who had enjoyed it before us. There is just something magical about being free, having no time constraints or concerns and just having family fun, hearing the giggles, listening to the laughter and feeling the thrill of jumping into fresh, clean water.

ADVENTURING WITH CHILDREN WHO HAVE ADDITIONAL NEEDS

Both my children have additional needs that need to be considered and managed when going on an adventure. Lyla has Perthes' disease, a condition affecting the hip joints, which was a massive thing to overcome and limited our access to the outdoors as a family. Lyla stopped walking when she was three and needed to use a wheelchair. We were determined not to let this stop us from getting outdoors and looked for ways we could adapt, using different slings so that we could carry her.

Lyla is a determined little lady and still wanted to go up mountains. My husband and I therefore both had to get fitter to be able to carry her, and we tried to make our gear as lightweight as possible. Since turning seven, Lyla's disease has changed, her bones developing and getting stronger. She is now able to cover longer distances by herself.

My son has dyslexia and possible autism, which also require additional considerations when adventuring in the outdoors. Tristan likes to know what is

happening and needs time to be able to digest our plans, so weeks before a trip I will start to brief him, showing him clips on YouTube of the walk we intend to do so he knows what to expect. He finds the concept of time and duration hard to understand, so instead of giving him time or length references, I will explain it in relation to TV programme lengths that he is familiar with – ie it's the length of watching the Gruffalo, which is 30 minutes.

Instructions need to be given one at a time outdoors so as not to overwhelm him. We also need to make sure he's had full control over what's packed in his bag and the food he has available. If he gets confused or unsure, this can lead to anxiety, and he can get quite stressed, so keeping on top of this is essential.

ENSURING A POSITIVE EXPERIENCE

Co-ordinating and juggling family, jobs and getting outdoors can be difficult. The required skills of multi-tasking are taken to an extreme level when you are an adventurous family! This doesn't mean it cannot be done. It just means you need to be creative with your time. The key thing to having a great adventure, which I have learned through trial and error, is to ensure the priority is making it fun and enjoyable. One of the best ways to do this is by simply including the children in the planning and asking them what they'd like to do. Make sure never to push them too far out of their comfort zone or to the point of exhaustion. With both our children, we make sure we are adapting to their needs and understand and consider their emotions at every stage. This way, the experience remains a positive one. If all else fails, never underestimate the value of a good snack – a sweet treat always works wonders as a little bribery!

The Ward family's adventuring top tips

- Keep it fun and enjoyable.
- Plan an adventure that is achievable; start off smaller and build up.
- Be organised and have a plan B get-out, just in case.
- Make sure your equipment is effective, breathable and lightweight.
- Check the Mountain Weather Information Service before setting off and keep yourself updated.
- Do not be afraid to abort if things are not going to plan.
- Ensure your family like the food they are eating.
- Make sure that if you need to go to the toilet you go to the toilet; model this behaviour.
- Keep the pace slow and enjoyable (walk to the pace of the slowest person).
- Haribo or other nice sweets to enjoy along the way always help lighten the mood.

Hiking in the Negev
desert, Israel

BIGGER
ADVENTURES

Using a child carrier to carry our baby and the gear we need for a multi-day hiking and camping trip in the desert

OUR ADVENTURES

GO EPIC

We were 1km (0.6 miles) away from our wild camping spot. In the Negev desert, Israel, wild camping is only allowed in designated areas, to protect wildlife. There's nothing in these spaces, usually just a few rocks in a large circle and a sign indicating you'd arrived.

I knew this camping spot was within a valley basin, but when I reached the edge and looked down, my heart stopped. It was much steeper and rockier than I had imagined.

We'd already trekked for 9km (5.6 miles) in the blazing desert heat. The

bag on my back had been an exhausting deadweight and made it hard to manoeuvre as it messed with my balance. I'd not weighed it but knew it must be at least 15kg (33lb). I was not concerned for myself but for

my precious little toddler, who was currently perched in the baby carrier on Gil's back. I imagined the horror of Gil stumbling and seeing him and Rivi fall.

I felt in that moment that horrible wave of vulnerability you feel as a parent when you imagine something bad will happen to your children. I wanted to burst into tears, but I knew that wasn't going to help, so I took a few deep, slow breaths instead. We had no choice but to reach the campsite as that's where we'd find our water – buried in a secret place in advance, the location shared with us via a WhatsApp video.

'I'll go first,' I told Gil as we tied away our hiking poles to the side of our backpacks (it's dangerous to use them on descents), 'Please don't worry about me, even if I stumble. Your priority is going slow and focusing on your footing and Rivi.'

'I will, I promise,' Gil reassured me, sensing my unease.

Of course, on the descent, as we cautiously scrambled over rocks and loose gravel, I questioned if I was a bad parent. We hadn't seen anyone all day and were in the heart of the Negev desert, miles from civilisation. But then I remembered that these 'danger films' I played in my head always visited me in times of stress, and nothing came of them. Like when Rivi rushes out of the house too quickly, and I imagine she's about to be hit by a car. Or when I lose sight of her in the playground, and in a moment my mind screams at me that she's been snatched. Or all those days when she's at nursery and my phone rings – something terrible has happened (it's usually just a sales call)!

Danger is our worst fear as parents and carers, and it's unavoidable. It's also not so black and white. Sure, we were hiking down a steep valley wall, and the danger involved in this was obvious, but we had managed those risks. As I clambered down, I reminded myself that we were both experienced hikers with first aid qualifications. We were carrying all the kit we

⅄ Following the way markers on the Israel National Trail

⚕ Gil carried Rivi and the items we needed for her, while I carried our tent, sleeping bits and food

needed to deal with anything that might happen. We'd run through all the 'worst case scenarios' – falls, getting lost, snake bites, flash flooding, heat stroke – and knew how we'd handle them and who would be responsible for what. Clipped to my backpack was a GPS Garmin that we could use to call for immediate help if we needed it. We were both fully here, present, concentrating on what we were doing.

Rivi was going to be absolutely fine!

CAMPING IN THE PROPER WILDERNESS

We safely reached the bottom of the valley and, with aching legs, marched the final distance to the camping space. It was a relief to take our backpacks off. In mine, I was carrying our tent, sleeping bags, roll mats, clothes, cooking stove, food and first aid kit. Gil had Rivi and, in the storage space of the baby carrier, our snacks, nappies and the all-important Charlie Bear. We were both carrying 3.5 litres (6 pints) of water each.

We set up the tent quickly, and Rivi fell asleep in a few minutes – a perfectly timed late cap-nap that gave us space to finish unpacking, stretch out our complaining muscles and find our water.

For the next few hours, we just rested as a family. We made pasta for dinner and lit a fire; had an aimless wander around the beautiful valley

floor, soaking up the mountains; chatted, sat in silence and then snuggled down in our sleeping bags when the darkness and cold descended. It took Rivi a long time to stop wriggling about in excitement, but it didn't matter; there was nothing for us to rush to or do and plenty of stars out to keep us occupied.

As I drifted off to sleep in the desert's impossible quiet, I replayed the fantastic views and memorable moments from the day. I couldn't believe we were here making this dream happen. Getting to this point had been years in the making. Researching, rebuilding fitness, testing our limits, problem-solving and giving things a try, even if we didn't know if they were possible or not. All that combined had led us here as a family, taking on an adventure, proving that it's all still available to you, even as parents. If we could make this adventure happen with a child, it really did feel like anything would be possible!

THE PLAN

As soon as I'd known we'd be in Israel visiting my in-laws, I couldn't get the idea out of my head that I wanted to return to the desert. It'd been five years since Gil and I had finished hiking the Israel National Trail. I wanted to return to my favourite part – the desert – to spend time in nature, retracing our footsteps.

≫→ Setting up camp in a designated camping area

←« Nap time while Gil prepares a snack

Although taking the off-road buggy would have been the easiest option, it wasn't possible as the terrain was ever-changing, with lots of scrambles and climbs. Our only option was to use a carrier to transport Rivi (now a decent weight as a big 20-month toddler) with most of the other items in my rucksack. Packing light would be key.

We opted for a four-day trip; the first two days would be gentle hiking close to villages. This enabled us to trial-run all our gear, adjust to the heat and hiking, and take in some natural springs and the Dead Sea.

From here, we'd do a bigger two-day hike deeper into the desert. The designated wild camping spots and water caching took out any flexibility with this part our plan. We'd have to complete the full 10km (6.2-mile) hike in a day and then the same distance hiking out the next day.

This was the biggest adventure we'd attempted yet, but the build-up hadn't come with the usual stress, only excitement this time. We were now

pros at packing for adventures as a family and knew how to handle the challenges that would come our way. For food, we had granola and fruit for breakfast (eaten dry), pitta and peanut butter for lunches, snack bars and nuts (or dried fruit for Rivi) for in-between meals, and pasta and pesto for dinner.

The bags were packed, we strapped Rivi into her car seat and headed south from Gil's family home to the desert.

BIGGER ADVENTURES

The walk back to our car on the final day was the most difficult part of the adventure. By then, my shoulders were pretty bruised from carrying my giant bag. My body was tired from all the walking, and I desperately needed a shower. We all did ... it had been four days since the last!

The things I had been worried about turned out to all be fine. The first was whether I could physically manage the bag's weight and the

←« An evening fire from collected scraps of wood

»→ We finished our adventure with a stay in a Bedouin campsite where we enjoyed a feast and a much-needed shower

distances. I was grateful we'd planned an easy first few days to adjust and build confidence and I was stronger than I gave myself credit for – all that lugging a baby around had counted for something!

The other thing that worried me was how Rivi would fare being in the carrier so much. Even a short walk at home can feel like too much if she's having one of those days when she hates being in the carrier. She surprised me on this trip. Of course, we had lots of stops, but she did more time in the carrier than ever before, almost entirely without fuss. The only occasion that she kicked off was less than an hour before we reached the car on the last day. We could see the end point in the distance, but nothing would chill her out. We took a break, and threw snacks, a dummy and songs at her, but she was having none of it. We had no choice but to strap her in and make the stressful romp to the car as quickly as possible while she complained. It made for a bit of an anticlimactic end to the adventure,

although thankfully we'd decided to treat ourselves and had booked a Bedouin tent to stay in that night. We showered, ate excessive amounts of food, Rivi made friends with a camel, and we celebrated with the few other hikers who were also staying there.

We always celebrate our wins at the end of an adventure. This had been a big one for our family!

TAKING ON A BIGGER
ADVENTURE

A 'big adventure' will mean different things to different families. Generally, though, it could be defined as travelling to somewhere more remote and challenging, covering longer distances or adventuring for extended periods of time.

It can be daunting thinking about going from doing microadventures close to home to bigger expeditions further afield. While some things will be different – you'll need more money, time and planning – the fundamentals remain the same. As someone who has done multiple long-distance treks (my longest lasting two months), I can assure you that it is not

much different from doing a single overnight trek. The equipment needed and the skills required are the same for both.

One of the hardest challenges to overcome with bigger adventures is getting over the mindset of believing it is possible and that you can make it happen. While we've all heard of families who do these crazy adventures – the neighbour who takes their children on a three-month safari through Africa or a family from school who spent their holidays walking the Camino de Santiago – it's not commonplace. It feels like a pipe dream that is out of reach, so big that you can't quite work out where to start.

Before having Rivi, my husband and I decided to kick-scoot the length of the USA, starting in Vancouver in Canada and finishing in Tijuana, Mexico. When I say we used a kick-scooter, I mean a non-motorised scooter, the same as your kids probably own, only a bigger, sturdier version. We came up with this challenge while looking for something epic that had never

⚓ Rivi watching camels from outside our Bedouin campsite

been done before. There was a lot of improvisation involved. We had to adapt the scooters to fit a pannier to the handlebars to carry our gear. Initially, we intended to follow the West Coast bike trail but had to adapt this as we realised some stretches were just too hilly for a kick-scooter. Each day, we improvised our accommodation for that night, sometimes staying with hosts (I'd ask in local Facebook groups) or finding gardens to camp in via the cycle tourists Warm Showers network (www.warm-showers.org), camping in sites or in the wild, and on some days, we even knocked on random doors asking if we could sleep in strangers' gardens.

This approach involved a lot of uncertainty and nerves, and that was before even accounting for the worries around fitness, how the scooters would cope with the long distances (they were great) and how we'd manage being on the move like that for three months.

This was a huge undertaking and not one I'd necessarily try with children – definitely not at the pace we were going at and the daily distances we covered. But the learnings from big trips like this have enabled me to think outside the box when it comes to our capabilities as a family. I know that whatever mad adventure idea we dream up next, we will be able to find a way to make it happen. To think on our feet as we go and problem-solve when it's needed. You never look at a big adventure as a whole. Like any project, you break it down step-by-step, day-by-day and in time it will happen.

Top tips for big adventures with children

- Get organised: you'll need good lists covering gear you need to take, your plan (with plan Bs and Cs in place) and maybe also a budget.
- Give yourself a very easy start. You and your children will need time to acclimate, so don't put pressure on the early days of your adventure by trying to cover any distance.
- Fatigue is often a killer on big adventures and the biggest reason people quit early – it's tiring being on the move all the time. You and your children will get tired, so make sure you factor in lots of breaks (for adults, it's recommended one rest day a week, but for children, I'd suggest doubling this). If you're going for more than a month, you might want to factor in a much bigger break halfway, where you stay put for a week or more.
- Think about your children's needs beyond just their physical ones. Being away for a long time, especially in an alien environment, can mentally

strain children. You might want to consider how they may be able to stay in touch with friends to help them feel grounded and connected to home and how you might give them opportunities to play with other children.

• Seek out expert advice. Reach out to other families who have done big trips (find them by searching online for blogs and forums), pay to speak with an expert to help you with planning or maybe even pay for a guide (even if just for the first few days).

• It's a good idea to do a trial run with all your kit before doing the big adventure. It's an opportunity to test everything out and see if there's anything that needs changing or could be left behind.

• A back-up safety device like a GPS Garmin is a great bit of kit for you to have when doing bigger adventures. It tracks your movements and allows you to send messages and call for emergency help if needed.

WALKING THE LENGTH OF THE UK

by Ian Alderman

@Our Spectrum Adventures | www.ourspectrumadventures.com

IN 2022, WE SET OUT to create a world record, challenge people's opinions on autism and give our daughter a once-in-a-lifetime experience! Together, we would backpack 2,092km (1,300 miles) from the most northerly location of mainland Britain to the most southerly point. The journey would take nine months, changing us as a family and individuals for ever and inspiring people around the world to have their own adventure.

This is the story of how we completed something that most people thought was impossible!

OUTDOORS AS A WAY OF LIFE

For us, the outdoors is a way of life, not just a hobby. Being outdoors and being adventurous is how we live our lives, where we feel we belong and how we thrive. It is our passion.

Deciding to walk the length of the UK combined several huge aspects of our lives: charity, autism, adventure, the outdoors and home education.

I live with my wife Sarah and our daughter Eve (age eight) near Aberfoyle in the Loch Lomond & The Trossachs National Park, Scotland. We're very privileged to live in such a magnificent location. We moved to Scotland from Northamptonshire in 2010 to be closer to the wild and untamed landscapes. Four years later, Eve was born.

Eve is home-educated, a decision we made early in her life. It was an easy and natural decision, but one that we didn't take lightly. Home-education has allowed us to give her a tailored education to meet her specific and unique needs. It is helped by the fact that Sarah is a qualified and experienced teacher.

The biggest influence in our adult lives occurred when Eve was aged just one and was diagnosed with a tumour on her spine. The prognosis was poor, with a life expectancy of a few days. At the same time, Sarah was undergoing some medical investigations that turned out to also be cancer. She would leave the children's hospital to go to her appointments, returning later to be at Eve's bedside. Eve and Sarah have since made a full recovery, but the psychological effects will last a lifetime.

The other huge influence in our lives is that both Eve and I are autistic. We have a formal diagnosis of Autism Spectrum Disorder through the NHS. Together, we represent the two most underrepresented groups of autistic people in the UK: late-diagnosed adults and young females. We are proud to be members of this unique and diverse group.

We began hiking the West Highland Way just before the Covid pandemic hit the UK. The first national lockdown happened on the second day of our hike, forcing us to return home. Lockdown was hard for us, and we spent most of our time in the garden and discussing plans and ideas for the future.

It was during this time that Eve had the idea to backpack the length of the country. The conversation developed from there, with Eve involved at every stage. In the end, we agreed to start the walk at Dunnet Head (the most northerly point of mainland Britain) and end at Lizard Point (the most southerly point of mainland Britain) going via John o'Groats and Land's End. It would be a continuous walk or thru-hike of 2,092km (1,300 miles).

We chose to do the hike as a charity fundraiser for the National Autistic Society. The other reason was to try to get people to think differently about autism, challenging some of the stereotypes and highlighting the mental health awareness movement.

Because of our charity aims, we decided to use social media to document our journey in all its glorious and gory details. This decision created a chain of events that would lead us to be guests on live radio and being recognised wherever we went. The whole experience was incredible and surreal!

The attempt, if successful, would lead to Eve holding an unofficial world record as the youngest person to walk the length of the UK. We allowed ourselves six months to reach Lizard Point. In the end, it took us over nine months, but we made it. Eve now holds that record proudly in her hands!

SETTING OFF

There was a sense of excitement in the air in the months leading up to setting off. We were becoming active on social media, gaining sponsors and getting public attention. For a family who are inherently introverted, it was a difficult adjustment.

On 1 March 2022, we arrived at a bleak, cold and windswept Dunnet Head and set off walking. It was one of the best feelings of my life, and I hope Eve will remember it with the same level of feeling.

Physically, we felt ready as we already spent most of our time outdoors. We were going to treat the hike as a marathon, not a sprint. We would hike within our ability, stopping and starting where and when we wanted. This ultimate freedom allowed us to be flexible. This was one of the best decisions we made and one of the biggest pieces of advice I could give to anybody considering something similar. You simply can't approach something of this magnitude, with an eight-year-old autistic child, without being flexible and adaptable.

The first few weeks were psychologically tougher than I ever expected. On the third night, I cried in our tent uncontrollably, being comforted by Eve. I underestimated how much I would miss Sarah and the feeling of pressure from what we were attempting. That night, the weather was brutal. The trail that day was barely walkable due to mud and bogs that slid into the huge geos and the waves crashing against the cliffs created a deafening roar. It was an intense experience. We got through that night together, Eve proving her emotional resilience was stronger than mine.

At no point over the nine months was Eve 'forced' to continue the walk. Sarah and I continuously reminded her that she could stop and end the challenge whenever she wanted. Not once did she ever say she wanted to stop! Eve kept me going, and I kept going for her. Sarah was the rock that held us all together. As we hiked, our individual and collective confidence grew. We now feel stronger and closer as a family for embracing the hard times and knowing that this hike, like life in general, was never intended to be easy!

A DYNAMIC APPROACH TO LOGISTICS

As we were actively blogging our journey on social media, we gathered a large following of people who offered us support and assistance along the way. Without these people, their kindness and generosity, I believe we would not have completed the walk! In the early days, we accepted lots of help due to my lack of emotional regulation and the weather in Caithness being unusually harsh. One particular day we only walked a few miles due to 97km/h (60mph) gusts. Eve couldn't even stand up, and I struggled. It was two steps forward, one step back. Eve loved the whole experience and was oblivious to my internal struggles.

The logistics of the hike had to be dynamic. We refined our daily tasks, trying not to restrict ourselves to specific food types or daily mileage. From an autistic

perspective, this was a challenge. Eve was brilliant and took everything in her stride.

Our hiking distance was between 9.6 and 21km (6–13 miles) daily, depending on the terrain and weather. En route, we were invited into schools, met with people, businesses and charities, gave interviews to newspapers and podcasts, and even featured on BBC radio on more than one occasion. Being recognised by strangers who knew so much about us, I must admit, was uncomfortable. By the end of the hike, however, it was a way of life, and I thought nothing of talking to strangers about our walk. It was something that I started to enjoy.

We already had a lot of the equipment we needed for our hike before our walk. I would strongly advise anybody against spending a lot of money as what you think you need is not always what will work for you. Everyone is different.

Throughout the nine months, our accommodation changed depending on what was available, where we were and, of course, cost! Around the urban areas we used Airbnbs, although our favourite thing was definitely wild camping. Later in the hike, we invested in a camper van. This was a game-changer, especially for Sarah, allowing her more freedom and convenience to come and see us. We viewed it as an investment, allowing us to expand our outdoor activities in the future. We have big plans for the next few years.

Our food was hard to deal with on the trail. I strive for a predominantly plant-based diet; however we do not enforce this on Eve. It would be easy to live off chocolate bars and convenience food, but not for months on end. We had to come up with a better, healthier, long-term plan. Sarah began cooking healthy meals at home and then used our domestic dehydrator to dehydrate them. This had the benefit of being cheaper, and we could eat regular healthy, home-cooked meals on the trail. We would also carry packet pasta with some cheese, and other convenience food if we ran out of dehydrated meals or had to resupply en route.

When we passed a shop, we would buy fresh fruit or vegetables to eat immediately or supplement our other meals. Eve would regularly buy a cucumber and munch on it as we walked. For breakfast and lunch, we would snack or sit down and have a mini picnic. Dried fruit was great, along with salted peanuts and flapjacks. We didn't ban convenience food, just tried to balance it out with healthier options. But treats were essential. Eve chose a hot chocolate in the colder months and, as the seasons changed, moved on to ice cream!

STRENGTH AND RESILIENCE

The biggest emotional challenge Eve had was missing our pets. When we started the hike, we had two cats and a dog. Partway through the hike, our dog, Tilly, passed away in Eve's arms. It was heartbreaking in the extreme, and even writing this short paragraph, I feel the tears in my eyes as the screen becomes blurry. A day and a half after it happened, we were hiking again; the trail and outdoors are the best therapy.

The other emotional challenge we faced happened just days before we reached our end point at Lizard Point. My parents had come to see us to spur us on to cross the finish line when my mother had a huge stroke. We knew it was bad, and her chance of survival was just 10–15 per cent. We carried on hiking around hospital visitation hours. It was hard, as my mother didn't even recognise us. Happily, she has since made a full recovery!

When the hike ended after nine months, we had developed greater emotional and mental strength and resilience. The simple truth is, for us, less is more, and simplifying and minimising our way of life gives us a sense of well-being that we have never experienced before.

I truly believe that no amount of money can buy you happiness. Happiness must be found within. Being able to carry my physical life in a rucksack gave me the headspace to manage life and all its complexities and allowed us the ultimate sense of freedom.

We are a happy family living a simple life with less than we ever thought was needed!

A bad day on the road is better than a good day in the office

CAMPER VAN TOURING

by Richard Reid
....
@touringwiththekids

AS WE BOARDED the ferry in the small seaport town of Hirtshals on Denmark's northern coast, a wave of excitement and anxiety began to engulf us. We were embarking on our final approach to a country that would leave a profound impact in our hearts and open our minds to the sheer beauty of this magnificent planet. We were approaching Norway. Our mission: to reach the highest point in Europe!

Once we had securely parked our camper van in the ferry's hold, we made our way up to the family section of the ship and luckily managed to get the last table. Much to the kids' delight, it was perfectly positioned within sight of the onboard play area. The last thing you want on a semi-long crossing is three restless kids.

At this point, the ferry sat perfectly still in the calm waters of the sheltered harbour walls. But this wasn't to last. As the ropes to the dock were released, the ferry started to move slowly forwards, and the view of what was to come came into sight. The Skagerrak strait, an extension of the North Sea, was colliding with the outside of the harbour walls with tall, ferocious waves. As the ferry crept slowly forwards, leaving the harbour's peacefulness, it started to roll from side to side, progressively getting worse as we left the Danish coast behind.

CHANGING LIFE FOR EVER

Before I go any further, let me fill you in on how we got into this situation. In late 2018, we were living in Dumfries and Galloway, Scotland. Despite having a good job and a picturesque fisherman's cottage as our home, we were struggling to settle in this rural location. Not knowing what to do or where to move to, and after loads of discussions, Keira (my wife) jokingly made a comment that has changed the way we view life today: 'Let's just sell up and go travelling.'

And that was it. We put plans into action, bought a seven-berth motorhome, and spent just under six months travelling 22,530km (14,000 miles) through ten countries across Europe with our two children: Piper, then three, and Jack, then two. It was an incredible experience.

After returning to the UK, we bought a house near Carlisle in the north-west of England, sold our motorhome and soon settled into a routine. Piper and Jack were going to a good local school while Keira looked after our newest addition – Teddy, who was born not long after returning home – alongside Charlie, our chocolate Labrador.

As for me, I was working locally as a Senior Forest Manager, a position I had not long held. But with this promotion came more responsibility. I slowly found the ever-increasing workload and pressures taking their toll. No longer was I excited to start my day. Instead, I spent my time reminiscing and re-living the memories of our last trip over and over in my head. I craved that adventure with my family once again.

Three years after our initial trip and after many discussions with Keira, we agreed to hit the road once again, this time indefinitely. I handed in my notice at work. The weight was lifted, the planning for our trip commenced, and a renewed lust for life began.

We already owned a camper van that we self-converted from a former builders' van, but this needed some pretty major alterations to allow us to travel and live in it full-time. The following months were spent working, planning and rebuilding our camper van followed by more planning and rebuilding. And then, just like that, my last day at work came and went, our house was sold, and we moved into our little home on wheels, ready to explore the best Europe had to offer.

We took the ferry from Harwich to the Hook of Holland, which was plain sailing, and then spent the next three weeks exploring the Netherlands, northern Germany and Denmark before setting sail for Norway.

> '*Exploring Europe together was not a decision taken lightly, but inspired and influenced by our desire to feel alive, live life to the full and in the process make precious memories and lifelong bonds with our children.*'
> — Keira Reid

REACHING NORWAY

After a four-hour crossing from Hirtshals, we finally arrived in Larvik on Norway's south-eastern coast. And you'll be pleased to hear that none of us was seasick and the kids kept busy in the play area. Once the ferry was docked, we headed south along the E18 coastal road to our first overnight park-up in the small coastal town of Kragerø. Despite being tired, we decided to explore the lively town on foot (except for our youngest, Teddy, who enjoyed the walk from the comfort of his pram). Walking among the wooden-clad buildings coloured in red, orange, yellow and white with fragrant flower baskets hanging off the lower windows, we couldn't shake the feeling of happiness at being here in this extraordinary country.

Over the next three weeks, we headed west and then hugged the coastline north, stopping regularly at places that sparked our curiosity. The journey ended up being more than 3,300km (2,050 miles).

Norway is known for having some of the world's most impressive waterfalls, and we stopped and gazed in amazement at many, including the well-known Vøringfossen and Steinsdalsfossen. Still, it was a lesser-known, and some would say underappreciated, waterfall called Skjervsfossen that took our breath away the most. We parked up in the small roadside lay-by and got the kids dressed in waterproof jackets before taking the short walk to the waterfall's base. We got within touching distance, so close that we were getting soaked by the spray of its impressive 120m (394ft) drop as the water fell like thunder.

Our journey took us along the twisting fjord side roads and up into the mountains. But what goes up, which in this case was us, must come down. At times, we were high up on a steep mountain edge looking down to the distant fjord below. Now, I'm not fazed by heights, but even this had me (quite literally) on edge. Keira simply refused to look, but for me, it's these moments that make it an adventure.

GIFT OF TIME

There was one adventure along the way that we simply couldn't miss: visiting the Nigardsbreen Glacier. The journey took us up the Jostedalen valley and then past the Breheimsenteret Glacier Centre to the small car park. We opted, much to the kids' delight, to take a short boat ride over the icy glacier lake to start our hike to the viewing area.

Piper and Jack led the way over the smooth rocks that only a few centuries ago would've been under ice. We made it to the glacier's base and looked into the blue ice at very close range. It was, and still is, the most awe-inspiring moment of my life. These moments when time seems to stand still make me realise the impact of our life's choices. I've often thought my job as a parent and a husband is to provide, and by providing, I mean through money and financial stability, a roof over our heads, food on the table and clothes on our backs. But it's times like this, looking over this colossal glacier, that I remind myself that the most important thing we as parents need to provide is time: time to bond, time to get to know our children, time to experience life together and for us, the time for adventures. I hope this is something I never lose sight of.

We were now in the far reaches of Northern Europe, a place that the indigenous Sámi People call home. Best known for reindeer herding, it was this majestic animal that we were now looking out for. The kids were especially excited, and it wasn't long until we spotted our first. With huge antlers and luscious white fur, it was positioned perfectly just off the road as we drove past. From here on, we saw reindeer most days, including a couple of times in large herds.

This was it; we turned off the highway and on to the E69, which would take us through this rugged and rocky landscape as far north as possible by road. As we climbed to 307m (1,007ft) above sea level, we made our final approach; we were here at Nordkapp, also known as North Cape, the furthest point north of mainland Europe.

We had made it!

Now, let the adventure begin at the most Southerly Point: Tarifa, Spain...

LIFE ON THE ROAD WITH THREE KIDS

Our home on wheels has approximately 9.5m² (102ft²) of floor space; that's it! To comfortably live as a family of five and a dog, it's important to utilise the space effectively. And that means cutting down on what you can take with you. Compromise is key.

Two of our kids are at school age, so we have to home-school. Though the subjects are quite basic, switching from parent to teacher role isn't always easy, and they are more inclined to play up than they otherwise would be at school. We have a small list of subjects they need to complete during the week, but we don't have a set timetable as we like to have some flexibility with our travels.

Safety plays a major part in our life on the road. We don't often stay in campsites and spend most nights either in aires or wild camping; both come with risks. But don't get me wrong, out of the 14 countries we have explored, we have only ever had one 'bad' experience and that was in the UK. We do our research using a couple of parking apps, and our rule is: if we have a bad gut feeling about a place, we move on; simple.

Sometimes things don't always go to plan. When we were visiting Germany, Piper got a UTI and had to go to the hospital. The language barrier and the unknown factor of how their health system works made it a daunting process, but in the end it all went perfectly. We've found that most people are more than happy to help, whether you're in hospital or lost on the road. It's important not to panic; there's always a solution.

Life on the road with three kids is tough, but it is so rewarding. We do this because of those lazy mornings lying in bed together, the peaceful (or challenging) walks, and the time just spent together in each other's company. I've said it before, and I'll say it again: a bad day on the road is a lot better than a good day in the office.

Little bit up, little bit down

HIKING IN NEPAL

by Catherine Edsell FRGS

....
@Cathadventure

MY LIFE AS AN EXPEDITION LEADER has taken me to some of the remotest areas of the planet. I love the complete immersion, working with pioneering scientists, and being completely off-grid. I met my husband, Mark, in a far-flung rainforest in Indonesia (he was the expedition doctor), and in 2004 we had Olivia, our first child.

Initially, we continued to travel as a small family, trekking through the Dolomites, staying in longhouses in Borneo, and camper-vanning around Australia, and then Hannah was born. With two children and a husband with a very demanding job, my working life ground to a halt. And for the next few years, the nearest I got to the jungle was as a 'schools explainer' in the Palm House at Kew and the dried mango in aisle 12 in Sainsbury's!

Mark joined the Caudwell Xtreme Everest medical research expedition, a team of doctors conducting the largest high-altitude research project from Kathmandu to the summit of Everest, investigating the impact of low oxygen

levels on the body. So, leaving the warmth of family life for three months, he camped on an ice floe in Everest base camp while I stayed behind with Olivia, aged two, and Hannah, aged six months. I'm not sure whose job was more taxing – at least he got some sleep!

As the children grew up and started kindergarten at a local Steiner Waldorf school, I began my forays back into expedition leading, often with the kids in tow. It was important for me to find a way to manage both aspects of my life: my role as a mum and my need to explore, teach and learn about the natural world.

I believe that children are very adaptable, and if you, as the parent, are at ease with the situation, they generally are too. I branched out into the aquatic realm as a divemaster and coral reef ecologist, as it's far easier to take your kids to a beach than drag them through a rainforest.

RETURNING TO NEPAL WITH CHILDREN

Ten years after the first Extreme Everest expedition, a second one was announced. Mark chose not to be part of the research team. Instead, we would go to Nepal as a family, taking the children. We teamed up with the Wilson family – Mark's research partner, his wife and their three kids. The plan: to walk through the foothills of the Himalayas from Shivalaya to Namche Bazaar, a challenging trek over 15 days with an ascent profile that matched the height of Everest.

We would have to cross three passes: Deurali La at 2,705m (8,875ft), Lamjura La at 3,530m (11,580ft) and Thaksindo La at 3,701m (12,142ft). Once we reached Namche and celebrated our achievement in the historic Hotel Sherwi Khangba, we would head back to Lukla and fly back to Kathmandu.

These days, most trekkers fly into Lukla and trudge to Everest Base Camp, missing out on the picturesque rhododendron forests, the multiple ice-blue river crossings on wobbly suspension bridges and the grand glimpses of Everest and other snow-capped peaks from lush, green, fertile valleys.

Ours was the route Edmund Hillary, Tenzing Norgay and all the original summiteers would have taken before the construction of the high-altitude airport, and in my opinion, it is not only the perfect way to acclimatise but a rich cultural, stunningly beautiful journey.

There's an expression in Nepal – 'Nepali flat: little bit up, little bit down', which basically means there's no flat ground whatsoever. We were about to find out what that actually meant.

GETTING INTO THE SWING OF EXPEDITION LIFE

We arrived in Kathmandu and stayed at the lovely Summit Hotel in Patan. The kids enjoyed the pool while we set about organising all the relevant trekking permits. The Summit Hotel provided the logistics for the Extreme Everest expeditions and helped us with our permits. We had packed frugally and were not hiring a porter, choosing instead to carry all our own kit. The Wilsons'

youngest was already being carried in a backpack by his dad, so they did use a porter to help with their luggage. This was not always the boon it promised to be, as their porter was decidedly reluctant – not cut from the legendary Sherpa cloth!

With permits in hand, we hired a minibus to take us to Shivalaya. There is a public bus, but we felt that the journey of eight hours on perilous roads with vertiginous drop-offs was best embarked

on without the added cacophony of chickens, goats and more passengers than there were seats.

Even with this luxury, it was still one of the most hair-raising journeys of my life. Our main aim was to not scare the children, so as adults, we had to dig deep every time we were balancing on two wheels on the edge of a cliff.

After the initial planning, the beauty of this adventure was the absence of organisation. No booking.com, no tour guide's itinerary. Once we reached Shivalaya and found simple accommodation (there were two or three teahouses to choose from), we settled down for a meal of noodles and went to bed.

This was how the days went from here on in. Wake up, pack up sleeping bags, get dressed, have breakfast (some kind of pancake or fried bread), start walking, stop for snacks, carry on walking, reach a village and stop for lunch (usually noodle soup), carry on walking, reach a village and find somewhere to stay, have dinner (probably dal baht/lentils and rice), go to bed and repeat.

We didn't book anything in advance. We had a map and an idea of where we needed to get to each night to stay on schedule; the path was from village to village, so there wasn't really any way to get lost.

There was only one night when we struggled to find accommodation, having to walk further and higher than we had anticipated. Still, the children, once they knew that there was really no option other than to carry on, were amazing and walked brilliantly. It was heart-warming to see their serious little faces as we explained our situation and then watch as they switched into joy and camaraderie as they chatted their way up the hill.

On arrival, us adults were tired,

and the stress of not knowing where we would be able to sleep that night had created a certain amount of tension. The kids, however, dropped their bags and went to play football, then made up an elaborate play (with songs) and performed it to the captive audience of the other trekkers in the teahouse.

THE CHALLENGES OF HIKING WITH FIVE CHILDREN

Trekking with five children does have its challenges. To start with, it was just keeping a rhythm as every few minutes someone would want to stop, have a snack, tie their shoelaces, go to the toilet. There were blisters to contend with, uncomfortable backpacks, and being too cold one minute, too hot the next.

After the first hour of uphill walking, where we had achieved virtually no distance at all, my heart sank. Perhaps we had bitten off more than we could chew, perhaps this trek was too difficult for small children, but as I have always said to any participant of any expedition I've led over the years, if you just keep putting one foot in front of another you will get there.

We started a rule of 20 minutes. No one was allowed to stop until we had walked for 20 minutes. Then, we could take a good break, have a snack and sort out any issues. After the initial grumbling had subsided, this is how we managed the rest of the walk. It gave structure for the children and meant that we could actually cover some ground.

Children of any age are very strong and fit; just watch them in a playground! They run and climb for ages. The trick was to take their focus off the walking and keep their minds occupied. We played word games and made up quizzes,

and the children named every insect they saw (not scientific names – but alphabetically: Anthony the ant, Walter the wasp, etc.).

The best day was heading from the Tashindo La pass to Nunthala down through a gnarled, ancient rhododendron forest where the children formed a wolf pack, and for a couple of hours, we lost sight of them, just hearing them wolf howling to one another through the trees.

There were natural goals to spur us on, like crossing the Lamjura La pass (our reward was a huge swarm of dragonflies that were also taking the path of least resistance) and reaching our village for the night to scope out the best teahouse. Traversing the turbulent rivers multiple times on rickety swinging bridges was at first quite scary for some children (especially when others would take wicked glee in wobbling it further by jumping up and down). Still, by the end, all would skip across merrily and even cross with the packs of mules that were being herded up to Namche Bazaar (the kids named all of the mules, too).

SO HOW WAS IT REALLY?

It was definitely the toughest adventure my children have ever done. All children are different, and there were different triggers for all of them. Olivia was worst in the morning, especially if it involved an immediate climb (which it often did). She would groan like a cow mooing and would need one-to-one coaching to get through the initial resistance, but once she had a good stride going, she was as fast as me. (Faster, actually, as she wasn't carrying a full pack.)

Hannah was great in the mornings but started to flag as it got hotter. She would need constant renditions of 'The Grand Old Duke of York' to get her up the hills, or alternatively be allowed to tell me the intricate plot of a banal movie she had watched – as long as I feigned interest and she kept on talking, she'd walk up anything.

The Wilson children had their own tactics – one would sit down whenever possible, and the other would steam ahead and then exhaust himself; the baby, however, was a dream, happy in his backpack popping raisins, a dead weight for his dad though when he fell asleep.

Life is simple on an adventure like this; physically tired from the day's trek, everyone sleeps well, even when covered by a smelly yak blanket. The food is literally fuel, and a hot cup of sweet chai around a fire in the evening is a blissful thing.

Top tips for a happy trek

• Anchor the children into the daily routine. We gave each of the children a stuff-sack with all their own clothes, their head torch and their sleeping toy. Each night, they could 'set up home', choose their bed, lay out their sleeping bag and arrange their clothes for bed and the next day. This gave them security amid the unfamiliar.

• Invent songs you can sing in a round – complicated enough that they take a while to master, but not so complicated that people get cross. The kids spent hours composing their own.

• Dried fruit and nuts were given at 20-minute intervals. (We also found some great coconut biscuits once our trail mix supplies ran out.)

• Seek out local children – great lunch breaks were spent playing hide and seek around Mani walls, playing chess (a universal game), football, climbing trees and paddling in icy streams.

• During one stop in a working monastery, the children were served tea by a novice monk about their age. He lit the ghee lamps as they listened in awe to the whomping of the long brass horns played as part of the ceremony.

• The best bit of kit we brought on the trek was our Water-to-Go bottles. These have a special filter that allows you to drink from ANY water source. We filled our bottles from mountain streams, animal water pipes and teahouse bathrooms – no one was ill. In addition, we didn't have to worry about carrying more than a litre of water at a time or buying any plastic bottles.

When our track merged with the main trail from Lukla to Namche Bazaar, and we had to share the path with tens of other trekkers, the children asked if we could go back to the other path. They had appreciated the peace and simplicity of just being with our families.

Namche Bazaar was a crazy place full of hustle and bustle, but we did wake up to a complete covering of snow, which made it magical.

We flew back to Kathmandu – another heart-in-your-mouth kind of ride! Our plane launched off the side of the mountain, the trails we had walked flashing beneath us, giving us a sense of the epic scale of what we had achieved.

To this day, it is still our children's favourite adventure – if you can climb the height of Everest, then you can pretty much do anything you put your mind to!

Stats

Ages of children:
2, 6, 8, 10, 12
Ascent: 8,450m
(27,723ft)
Descent: 6,810m
(22,343ft)
Distance walked:
115km (72 miles)
**Hours walked per
day:** 7–8
Days walking: 13

Itinerary

Days 1–3:
Kathmandu
Day 4: Shivalaya
Day 5: Bhandhar
Day 6: Kenja
Day 7: Goyam
Day 8: Junbesi
Day 9: Ringmo
Day 10: Nunthala
Day 11: Karikhola
Day 12: Paiya

Day 13: Ghat
Days 14–15: Namche
Bazaar
Day 16: Phakding
Day 17: Lukla
Day 18: Kathmandu

SHORT-TERM EFFORT
FOR LONG-TERM GAIN

Pursuing outdoor family adventures is not something I see as just a hobby that I do on the side. It's a conscious choice. A lifestyle and parenting style that shares the values and qualities I want for all children. It represents what I see as wholesome parenting. The sort of dream vision that I had of how I'd raise a family – outdoors with muddy knees, moving our bodies, time in quiet spaces, close to nature, learning to distinguish between what is necessary in life and what are just 'things' that don't add value, and time together where we are fully present.

Outdoor adventures offer an antidote to our society that, in many ways, supports the complete opposite of what Gil and I, and I believe most parents, want for our children. It's too easy to fall into the trap of spending extended periods of time indoors, munching on unhealthy processed foods, overstimulating our children with soft plays and kids' parties, and never fully being present, as we're all distracted and addicted to our individual screens. These trappings often feel like the 'easy' options when parenting day-to-day. When your kid drives you crazy, putting them in front of cartoons offers instant relief and the break you desperately need and deserve. But it's a short-term gain that makes your life harder in the long run.

While getting outdoors initially seems like a lot of work – making a plan, packing, getting dressed and actually getting out the door – the benefits outweigh the efforts a million to one. I've seen with the children in my life

⚡ Enjoying a swim in a hidden oasis in the Negev desert, Israel

how that time in nature makes them easier to raise – they become calmer, more independent and less demanding. It's a short-term effort for long-term gain. It teaches them to be comfortable with long silences. To learn how to seek out their own games, even in relaxed, under-stimulating environments, without relying on an adult to provide constant activities and entertainment. Away from screens, adverts and media, they get to step away from the endless bombardments and pressure telling them how they should behave based on their gender at birth or what toy they have to own next to feel validated and worthy. They get to be with their family unit for a short time, working as a team towards the same goal. And perhaps the most beneficial factor? They get a parent who is present, relaxed, less stressed, and caring for their health and well-being ... because the evidence is overwhelmingly there. Getting active in nature has incredible benefits for us all!

One of the things I love most about running Love Her Wild is that I get to witness the catalyst for change that going on adventures brings many. Sometimes that's personal – growing in confidence and realising what you're truly capable of. Sometimes it's practical – changing jobs, leaving situations behind or pursuing a dream pushed aside for too long.

Adventures are magic. They are healing, creative and exciting. Just because you've made the bold and beautiful decision to have children doesn't mean you have to leave that all behind. As with all areas of parenting, you just have to adapt and slow down, and anything is still possible.

It's never too late to change your narrative. If you have the desire to get outdoors more with your family, stop listening to the naysayers and start owning the changes that need to happen to make that possible. No adventure is too small to be worthwhile. Start taking those small steps together as a family. Remember to keep being patient and kind to yourselves ... it's a journey and not a linear one at that. Family adventures get considerably easier as your children get older, so those first steps are just about you all learning how this works while building some priceless memories.

This book is full of incredible families going against the grain and making family adventures a fabric of their lives. Hold that inspiration and start actioning it into a plan – don't let it fizzle away as we too often do with our dreams. There are many adventures waiting for you and your family ... who knows where they will take you?!

⚑ Adventuring with friends can make trips a lot more fun for children

FAMILY-FRIENDLY ADVENTURE COMMUNITIES

Blaze Trails
www.blazetrails.org.uk
Empowering parents to get outdoors with their babies.

Family Camping UK
Facebook group
For families who enjoy the great outdoors. It doesn't matter what your camping style is, whether it's a hammock, tent or camper van.

Outdoor Mums UK
www.outdoormums.com
A vibrant community where families can share their adventures, favourite locations and outdoor activities, seek advice and encourage and support one another.

Family Cycling UK
Facebook group
A group for chat and campaigning for anyone who has ever ridden a bike with kids or wished they could.

Single Parents Camping UK
Facebook group
A group to share hints, tips, locations and possibly even hook up to help get kiddies out into our beautiful countryside.

Ordinary Superparents
Facebook group
Find adventure in everyday family life – learn, grow and build happiness.

GAMES AND ACTIVITIES

Knowing a couple of games and activities can make all the difference on an adventure when you're faced with tired, grumpy or bored children. A quick game can change their energy in minutes and save you from full-on meltdowns.

Here's a collection of some of my favourite games and activities to do outdoors. They are suitable for children of all ages and don't require any specialist equipment. And don't forget, it's much more fun for your little ones (and for you) if the adults join in too.

Credit: I picked up most of these games from attending and volunteering for ATE Superweeks. ATE Superweeks is a charity providing residential summer camps for children aged 8 to 16 in the UK. Find out more: www.superweeks.co.uk

KEYWORD (GAME)

Choose a keyword – it's even better if you let your children decide what it'll be (to explain, let's say our keyword is 'dog'). Carry on your conversation as usual, and at some point, drop in the word dog. As soon as you've said it, close your eyes and start counting to ten. Everyone has until ten to hide out of sight. On ten, you open your eyes – if you can see anyone, they have not won the round.

This is a great game to keep playing throughout your adventure, dropping your keyword when everyone least expects it, such as at mealtimes or when relaxing in the tent. You can also mix up whose turn it is to say the keyword (although I warn you that most children will be making you run and hide every minute!).

10 SECONDS (GAME)

This is my go-to game, as you can play it anywhere and adapt your tasks to make it age-appropriate. All players must be touching your hand. You then give a command and count to ten. The players have to complete the task by the time you reach ten.

Ideas for tasks are: bring me three different types of leaves, touch something blue, hug a tree, stand on one leg in a puddle, bring me a stick longer than your arm, balance on a tree stump or touch something smooth.

SCAVENGER HUNT (ACTIVITY)

Before heading out, create a scavenger hunt. On a piece of paper, list items that you need to find (ie moss, large rock, squirrel, brown leaf, mushroom, flower, tree stump, fern, acorn, feather). Once spotted, tick them off the sheet until you've found them all.

MAKE A LEAF MANDALA OR PICTURE (ACTIVITY)

A great little activity in autumn is collecting different-coloured leaves and then working together to create a large mandala or picture.

FRUITS (GAME)

This is another nice game to play throughout an adventure. You don't need to be playing the game constantly but can dip in and out of it throughout the day to catch the next player out. All players choose for themselves the name of a piece of fruit. The player who is 'on' must attempt to say another player's fruit three times – 'apple, apple, apple' – before the target can say it once. If they succeed, the named player is now 'on'. If they fail, the original player remains 'on' and must try again with the same or a different fruit.

The players will soon realise that the fruits with the longer syllables are harder to catch out, so you may want to switch each player's fruits once they under-stand the game (unless you think that'll be part of the fun). They will also learn that it's best to catch a player out while they're distracted in a task or mid-conversation.

NATURE SCULPTURE (ACTIVITY)

Using pebbles, leaves, twigs and anything else you can find in nature, create sculptures of animals. You can give younger children an idea of an animal to start with. For older players, you can make it a competition by keeping your animal a secret and then having to guess what each other's animal is.

A–Z CHALLENGE (GAME)

Take it in turns to make your way through the alphabet. When it's your turn, you have to say an item you've seen on your adventure that begins with that letter (a – apple, b – branch, c – cow, etc.) If a player gets stuck, everyone can pitch in to help.

BUILD A DEN (ACTIVITY)

A timeless classic! Work together to build a den, then step inside for a snack or picnic. Remember to dismantle the den when you've finished, returning the branches and leaves to the ground where you found them.

LEAF AND BARK RUBBINGS (ACTIVITY)

For this activity, you'll need thin paper and a large wax crayon or piece of charcoal. Placing your paper over a leaf (laid down on a flat surface) or section of bark, rub the crayon or charcoal back and forth until you've created a rubbing on the paper. Collect as many different ones as you can. When you return home, you can cut them up and use glue to create a mosaic of all the different textures.

ANIMAL NOISES (GAME)

This is one of my favourite games. It's silly and can easily be used to lighten the mood around a campfire or on a break on a walk. You need at least four players, all over the age of four.

Someone is blindfolded (or closes their eyes) and stands in the middle. Everyone starts to walk around the person in a circle. Alternatively, you can have someone spin around the person in the middle until they are disorientated. The person in the middle will shout stop, and everyone has to stand still. The person in the middle will then randomly point and say the name of an animal. The person they point at (or whoever is closest) will then have to make the sound of the animal. If the person in the middle can guess correctly who made the noise, they swap with them. Otherwise, they keep going for another round.

THE FLOOR IS LAVA (GAME)

When you're in a good location (such as woodland), shout 'the floor is lava' and begin counting down from five. Everyone has five seconds to get both their feet off the ground in any way possible, be it hanging from a branch or perching on a log. At the end of five seconds, if someone still has any contact with the ground, they lose and are next to shout 'the floor is lava'. If everyone is successful, you continue to be the caller.

The game can be played continually on an adventure at random moments, but you may wish to remain the caller, so you ensure it only happens in safe spaces.

GUIDED MISSILES (GAME)

This game is for only four players, but it's fun to watch if you also have spectators. Two players are blindfolded and put near each other (but not touching) – these are the missiles. Each missile is given another player who is their guide – the guide must sit or stand still.

A small circle is drawn in the mud, or an object (such as a leaf) is laid on the floor nearby. Each guide takes turns to give an instruction to their missile. This can be a direction followed by a number of steps but nothing more. For example, 'turn right and take three small steps'.

The winning team is the first missile to get entirely in the circle or with part of their foot touching the allocated object.

HALT (GAME)

Pick two players, who stand back to back. At a signal, they both start walking until you shout 'halt' – on this command, they both stop and face each other. The game is to estimate the least number of strides it would take to reach the other player. The aim is to underbid the person you are playing against.

Pick a player who needs to give the first estimate. The other player can then bid a lower number, or if they don't think it's possible to make the distance in that number of strides, say, 'prove it'.

If your opponent says, 'prove it,' you must then try and make the distance in the lowest number that you bid. If you make it, you win. If not, your opponent wins. You can keep switching if you have more players, with the winner staying on.

CAMPFIRE BREAD ON A STICK (ACTIVITY)

If you have access to a fire, this little recipe is a great activity to do as a family. You'll need the following ingredients:

- 1 mug of self-raising flour
- A pinch of salt
- (optional) 2 tablespoons of oil
- 250ml of water, milk or plant milk
- (optional) extras for flavours – garlic, rosemary, olives, dried fruit or chocolate chips

Mix the flour, salt and oil together, then slowly add the water/milk/plant milk. Knead your dough for around five to ten minutes, then add any extra flavourings and knead so they are evenly distributed. The more you knead it, the lighter and fluffier your breadsticks will be.

Task your children with finding long, thin sticks. Take a handful of dough, roll it into a skinny snake and wrap it around the end of the stick in a spiral. Put it over the fire, twisting regularly until the bread is cooked evenly.

INDEX

PICTURE CREDITS

All photographs © Bex Band, with the exception of:

(T = Top / B = Bottom) © **Adobe Stock**: 39, 41 (BR), 45, 49, 105, 107, 125, 134–5, 147–9, 155–7, 164, 167, 168, 182, 183–6, 203, 205B, 206B, 211, 244, 245, 246, 247, 249, 256–9, 266, 267, 308, 312, 316, 320; © **Alice Somerset and Dave Pearson-Smith**: 194–202; © **Alistair Ross**: 158–63; © **Charlie Ward**: 4, 268–73; © **Che Ramsden**: 126–30; © **Craig Moffat**: 136–41; © **Gareth Davies**: 260–5; © **Getty**: 101, 165, 204, 205T, 206T, 208, 309, 311; © **Ian Alderman**: 288–93; © **Kerry-Anne Martin**: 31, 92–7; © **Laura Bridger**: 6–7, 108–11; © **Leanne Woodall**: 150–3; © **Mark Edsell**: 300, 301, 302, 304T, 305, 307; © **Mark Wilson**: 303, 304B, 306; © **Neil Muir**: 169–73; © **Nisbah Hussain**: 73–7; © **Peak UK**: 234, 235; © **Rachel Healey**: 212–19; © **Richard Reid**: 294–9; © **Samantha Fletcher**: 54–9; © **Sarah White**: 68–72; © **Simon Margot**: 250–5; © **Tim Moss**: 34–8; © **Tobina Marx**: 238–43; © **Trev Worsey**: 2–3, 190–3

ACKNOWLEDGEMENTS

This was a tough book to write! While writing and editing, I sat in coffee shops, trying to ignore the unbearable itch to get out adventuring. That constant source of inspiration was all thanks to my incredible contributors, who kindly shared their family adventures. Your stories have brought this book to life.

It was also a period in my life with various unforeseen challenges to overcome, making the writing process that much harder. Thank you to my wonderful friends who supported me through those rocky waters, most notably Emma, Seanna, Laura, Ella, Trina, Libby and Lucy.

If you've not been to my local independent bookshop, Winstone's Hunting Raven Books in Frome, you should. I discovered the manager isn't just great at giving good book recommendations, but also happy to be on hand for publishing meltdowns and advice … thanks Tina.

I'm so grateful to the team at Bloomsbury for seeing the need to get this book into parents' hands, especially to my talented editor, Jenny Clark. I hope I did you proud!

Finally, the biggest thanks go to my unbeatable husband Gil and my gorgeous daughter Rivi. And to my wonderful niece and nephew, Dulcie and Cooper. Here's to many more years of adventuring together!